2025

Mittlerer Schulabschluss

Original-Prüfungsaufgaben und Training

Nordrhein-Westfalen

Englisch 10. Klasse

LÖSUNGEN

STARK

Bildnachweis

S. 22: Hintergrund: © 123rf.com; Kiwi: © Eric Isselee. 123rf.com
S. 28: © Amiami3, lizenziert unter CC BY-SA 3.0

18. ergänzte Auflage
www.stark-verlag.de

Inhalt

Vorwort

Lösungen zu den Übungsaufgaben der Kompetenzbereiche

▶ **Lösungen zum Hörverstehen** **2**

Listening Test 1: Robben Island 2
Listening Test 2: The News 3
Listening Test 3: Apple and Rain 4
Listening Test 4: Grey Owl 6
Listening Test 5: The Art of Being Normal 7
Listening Test 6: The California Gold Rush 8
Listening Test 7: The Stolen Generations 9
Listening Test 8: Couchsurfing or Wilderness? 11
Listening Test 9: Inventing Elliot 11
Listening Test 10: Sandringham 12
Listening Test 11: The Super Bowl 13
Listening Test 12: Sundae Girl 15
Listening Test 13: Mary Robinson 16
Listening Test 14: New Zealand Tips 17

▶ **Lösungen zum Leseverstehen** **18**

Reading Test 1: The Kiwi – New Zealand's Iconic Bird 18
Reading Test 2: Young Refugees Learn about U.S. on the Soccer Field 23
Reading Test 3: The History of Halloween 25
Reading Test 4: Getting to Know Canada 27
Reading Test 5: Volunteering in Australia 30
Reading Test 6: "We May Be 'Born Free', but ..." 31
Reading Test 7: School Life Abroad 33
Reading Test 8: The Double Life of Cassiel Roadnight 34
Reading Test 9: Boot Camps for Teenagers 36
Reading Test 10: Bog Child 37

▶ **Lösungen zum Bereich Wortschatz – Verfügbarkeit sprachlicher Mittel** **39**

▶ **Lösungen zum Bereich Grammatik – Sprachliche Korrektheit** **48**

▶ **Lösungen zum Schreiben** **61**

Allgemeine Übungsaufgaben zum Bereich „Schreiben" 61

Spezielle Übungen zu textgebundenen Schreibaufgaben 73

Lösungen zu den Original-Aufgaben der zentralen Prüfung in NRW

▶ **Mittlerer Schulabschluss 2019** **2019-1**

▶ **Mittlerer Schulabschluss 2021** **2021-1**

▶ **Mittlerer Schulabschluss 2022** **2022-1**

▶ **Mittlerer Schulabschluss 2023** **2023-1**

Mittlerer Schulabschluss 2024 ...... **www.stark-verlag.de/mystark**

Sobald die Original-Prüfungsaufgaben 2024 freigegeben sind, können die zugehörigen Lösungen als PDF auf der Plattform **MySTARK** heruntergeladen werden (Zugangscode vgl. Umschlaginnenseite).

Lösungsvorschläge erstellt von:

Patrick Charles, Walter Düringer, Paul Jenkinson, Sandra Klüser-Hanné, Elke Lüdeke, Redaktion (Übungsaufgaben)

Martin Paeslack (Lösungen der Prüfungsaufgaben, Übungsaufgaben)

Vorwort

Liebe Schülerin, lieber Schüler,

dieses Buch ist der Lösungsband zu „Original-Prüfungen und Training – Mittlerer Schulabschluss 2025 – Englisch – NRW“ (Best.-Nr. J05150). Es enthält ausführliche und kommentierte Lösungsvorschläge zu den Übungsaufgaben und zu den Prüfungsaufgaben der letzten Jahre.

Die Lösungen ermöglichen es dir, deine Leistung einzuschätzen. Es handelt sich um **Lösungsvorschläge**, die dir zeigen, wie man die Aufgaben richtig und umfassend beantworten kann. Das heißt, dass – außer bei den geschlossenen Aufgaben – auch andere Lösungen als die hier abgedruckten möglich sind. Die Lösungsvorschläge im Bereich „Schreiben“ sind manchmal ausführlicher als gefordert, um dir Anregungen zu geben, was du alles schreiben könntest. Das heißt nicht, dass deine Antworten auch immer so lang sein müssen. Wichtig ist, dass du die Hinweise beachtest, die in der Aufgabenstellung genannt sind, und alles **vollständig** und **richtig** bearbeitest.

Außerdem gilt: Versuche stets, die Aufgabe zunächst **selbstständig** zu lösen, und sieh nicht gleich in der Lösung nach. Solltest du nicht weiterkommen, helfen dir die grau markierten **Hinweise und Tipps** vor der jeweiligen Lösung. Wenn du sie gelesen hast, solltest du unbedingt selbstständig weiterarbeiten. Am Schluss solltest du deine Lösung in jedem Fall mit der angebotenen Lösung vergleichen sowie deine eigenen Ergebnisse kontrollieren und korrigieren oder ergänzen. Lies zu allen Aufgaben, die du nicht richtig lösen konntest oder bei denen du dir unsicher warst, noch einmal die allgemeinen Erläuterungen in dem entsprechenden Kapitel im Trainingsband.

Viel Spaß beim Üben und vor allem viel Erfolg in der Prüfung!

▶ Lösungen zu den Übungsaufgaben der Kompetenzbereiche

Lösungen zum Hörverstehen

Allgemeiner Hinweis: Zu Übungszwecken kannst du dir die Hörtexte so oft anhören, wie du möchtest. Wenn du die Aufgaben unter Prüfungsbedingungen bearbeiten möchtest, solltest du dir den jeweiligen Text aber nur zweimal anhören. Lies den Hörverstehenstext nur durch, wenn du mit den Lösungen ganz unsicher bist und gar nicht weiterkommst.

Listening Test 1: Robben Island

1. ... 30-minute boat journey.
   Hinweis: "It takes about 30 minutes to get there by boat." (Z. 10)

2. to show you/visitors/people around
   or: to tell you/visitors/people stories about the conditions there
   Hinweis: "The prison is now a museum but you can only visit it with a guided tour where former prisoners show you around and tell you stories about the conditions there." (Z. 13–15)

3. ... ex-guards.
   or: ... former guards.
   Hinweis: "... most of the ex-prisoners still live on Robben Island and some of their ex-guards do, too." (Z. 15/16)

4. ... for political prisoners.
   Hinweis: "... the maximum-security prison was not for bank robbers or anyone like that, but for political prisoners." (Z. 21/22)

5. ... were not allowed to mix.
   Hinweis: "... they were locked up in dormitories – large rooms, which had about 40 people in each one. These were for 'normal' political prisoners – the leaders, like Nelson Mandela, had single cells and were separated from the others." (Z. 28–31)

6. … helped each other and talked a lot.
   ✎ *Hinweis: "Many prisoners couldn't read or write when they arrived on Robben Island, so those people who could taught the others. They also formed small groups to discuss political issues …" (Z. 33–35)*

7. at the doctor's
   or: inside tennis balls
   ✎ *Hinweis: "The doctor […] came every Wednesday – leaders and group heads often pretended to be ill on those days, and while waiting for the doctor they came into contact with each other. Sometimes, the messages were also put into tennis balls and 'accidentally' hit over the separating wall." (Z. 39–43)*

8. … accepted anything the other prisoners wouldn't also get.
   ✎ *Hinweis: "If he was offered a privilege, he wouldn't accept it unless all the other prisoners got it, too." (Z. 47/48)*

9. sea is very cold
   or: strong currents (in the sea)
   or: many sharks (in the sea)
   ✎ *Hinweis: "… you would probably have died trying to swim to the mainland. The sea is very cold, and there are strong currents and many sharks." (Z. 52–54)*

Listening Test 2: The News

News Item 1: The Pardoning of the Thanksgiving turkey

1. … Pilgrims' first harvest.
   ✎ *Hinweis: "Its origins can be traced back to the time of the Pilgrim Fathers […] who celebrated their first successful harvest." (Z. 2–4)*

2. … was given a turkey as a present.
   ✎ *Hinweis: "Harry Truman was the first president to be presented with a turkey as a gift to his family …" (Z. 9/10)*

3. ... Ronald Reagan.
   Hinweis: "The first time an official pardon was issued took place in 1987, when Ronald Reagan was asked ..." (Z. 15/16)

4. ... was indirectly responsible for the first turkey pardoning.
   Hinweis: "... Ronald Reagan was asked whether he would pardon Oliver North, a man who was engaged in the so-called 'Iran-Contra Affair', a political scandal during Reagan's presidency. As he did not want to answer the question, he preferred to pardon the turkey instead ..." (Z. 16–19)

News Item 2: What about a Batmobile?

1. ... is 29 years old.
   Hinweis: "This might be the line of thoughts that crossed 29-year-old Australian Zac Mihajlovic's mind a few years ago." (Z. 24/25) Zac lebt nicht in Österreich („Austria"), sondern in Australien, und er ist auch nicht 1998 geboren (im Text kommt lediglich die Zahl „1989" vor, vgl. Z. 27).

2. ... in his backyard.
   Hinweis: "He spent two years of his life building an exact copy of the Batmobile shown in the first movie from 1989 in his backyard." (Z. 26/27)

3. ... it has a real car licence.
   Hinweis: "It took Zac another year to work in all the details needed for a registered car licence. Now the car is not just a life-sized model – it is actually driving with licence plates, papers and all." (Z. 27–30)

4. ... there were people blocking his way.
   Hinweis: "Once he even needed a police escort to get out of a place when he was in Sydney with the car." (Z. 34/35)

Listening Test 3: Apple and Rain

1. ... after a lesson.
   Hinweis: "[Sound of a school bell ringing.] *'Good work today, folks. See you tomorrow,' Mr. Gaydon says, giving us permission to pile out of the classroom into the heaving corridor." (Z. 1–3)*

Hier kannst du auch aus den Hintergrundgeräuschen (Gong; Schüler im Gang) erschließen, dass die Situation nach einer Schulstunde stattfinden muss.

2. … a fun day out.
   ✎ *Hinweis: "'We went swimming on Sunday and there were these guys there who …,' Donna begins, but she can't continue because she is laughing again. Uncontrollably." (Z. 10–12)*

3. … did not know they were going.
   ✎ *Hinweis: "'You went swimming together?' I ask. Pilar didn't tell me. She certainly didn't invite me." (Z. 13/14)*

4. … feels they do not want her there.
   ✎ *Hinweis: "'Shall we get lunch, Pilar?' Donna asks. She doesn't look at me, so I know I'm not invited …" (Z. 24/25); "'You hungry, Apple?' Pilar asks uncomfortably. Donna sighs. Hazel rolls her eyes. Mariah walks away." (Z. 27/28)*

5. … afraid of losing her only friend.
   ✎ *Hinweis: "Pilar's my only friend. If I lose her, I'll have no one." (Z. 38/39); "I don't want anyone knowing I've got no friends." (Z. 45/46)*

6. hide in the toilets
   or: go to the office/nurse and say she is sick
   ✎ *Hinweis: "I can hide out in some toilets until school finishes …" (Z. 48/49); "… I could go to the office and say I'm sick." (Z. 51)*

7. … disappointments in a friendship.
   ✎ *Hinweis: Bei dieser Aufgabe musst du entscheiden, welches der drei Satzenden den Romanauszug am besten zusammenfasst. Im Text werden zwar verschiedene Freizeitaktivitäten genannt (z. B. schwimmen gehen), das ist aber nicht das zentrale Thema. Auch schulische Probleme stehen nicht im Vordergrund. Das Kernthema des Textes ist vielmehr Apples Enttäuschung über ihre Freundin Pilar, die sich mit einer neuen Clique abgibt, in der Apple nicht willkommen ist.*

Listening Test 4: Grey Owl

1. … half-Apache.
   Hinweis: "Grey Owl claimed that he was half-Apache …" (Z. 4/5)

2. … catch beavers for their fur.
   Hinweis: "At 17, he left home to be a trapper in Canada, catching beavers for their fur." (Z. 10/11)

3. … he had blue eyes.
   Hinweis: "Unlike most indigenous people, however, Archie had blue eyes. But when the other trappers asked him about his identity, he always told them that his father was Scottish …" (Z. 13–15)

4. … by a tribal chief.
   Hinweis: "During his travels in Canada, he was rescued from snow blindness by a tribal chief who then taught him more about how to survive in the wilderness." (Z. 24–26)

5. … he was told to bring two young beavers home.
   Hinweis: "One day he'd killed a beaver but left its young behind alone, which would have meant certain death for them. His wife thought this was cruel so she made him bring the two beaver babies home where they raised them by hand. From that moment, his whole life changed." (Z. 30–34)

6. … protecting wildlife.
   or: … conservation.
   Hinweis: "He quit trapping and began writing books about protecting wildlife." (Z. 36)

7. … was invited to talk to the Royal Family in Britain.
   Hinweis: "By that time, he'd become so famous as a conservationist, he even gave a talk to the Royal Family in Buckingham Palace." (Z. 42–44)

8. … the press …
   Hinweis: "… soon after he died in 1938, the press found out that Grey Owl, the supposed half-Apache, was really an Englishman named Archie Belaney." (Z. 46–48)

9. ... he hadn't told the truth about himself.
✎ Hinweis: "... people were angry because of the lie. Some bookshops stopped selling his books, and others only sold ones with his real name on. Many indigenous people are still very angry that he pretended to be one of them." (Z. 52–54)

Listening Test 5: The Art of Being Normal

1. ... has already heard about Becky's party.
✎ Hinweis: "'Are you going to Becky's party?' [Alicia] asks slowly. 'I didn't know she was having one,' I reply. This isn't quite true. Becky Somerville is in my form and has such a big mouth you'd have to be living on Mars not to have heard her go on about it." (Z. 10–13)

2. ... does not really like parties.
✎ Hinweis: "I dunno. Parties aren't really my scene." (Z. 17)

3. ... are a bit afraid of Leo.
✎ Hinweis: "Becky treats me like most of my other classmates seem to, with this mixture of fear and fascination, like I'm an exotic animal escaped from the zoo that may or may not be dangerous." (Z. 27–29)

4. ... feel rather insecure.
✎ Hinweis: "'I'm just not great at crowds,' I add. I regret my words straight away because I know I'm making it worse, blowing it big-time with my weirdness." (Z. 23/24)

5. ... she understands what he feels like.
✎ Hinweis: Alicia merkt, dass Leo eher unsicher ist. Da sie selbst einmal neu an der Schule war, kann sie gut nachvollziehen, wie er sich fühlt (vgl. Z. 34–48).

6. ... seems well-integrated at Eden Park School.
✎ Hinweis: Alicia hat schnell Anschluss gefunden, indem sie aktiv auf andere Schüler zugegangen ist und bei diversen Schulaktivitäten mitgemacht hat. Sie scheint gut an der Schule integriert zu sein und viele Freunde zu haben (vgl. Z. 46–48).

7. ... go to the party with Leo.
Hinweis: Hier musst du ganz genau hinhören: Alicia fragt Leo nicht direkt, ob er mit ihr auf die Party gehen will, sondern umschreibt ihren Wunsch lediglich (vgl. Z. 50–54). Ruby packt die Äußerungen ihrer Freundin Alicia aber noch einmal in etwas deutlichere Worte und „übersetzt" sie für Leo: "Leo, Alicia is trying to ask you out" (Z. 57/58).

8. ... happy and excited because he will go to the party with Alicia.
Hinweis: "'Er, yeah, OK then.' I find myself saying, my steady voice fighting my motoring heartbeat and sweaty palms." (Z. 63/64); "... suddenly I'm doing something I haven't done in forever, and it's like I'm having this weird, out-of-body experience – because I'm laughing too." (Z. 66–68)

Listening Test 6: The California Gold Rush

1. ... a settler.
Hinweis: "... thousands traveled west to California after a settler reported finding gold there." (Z. 2/3)

2. ... a river.
Hinweis: "Mr. Marshall was building a sawmill near the American River in central California. When he looked in the water, he saw shiny pieces of metal." (Z. 4–6)

3. (Mr. Marshall) bit down on it
or: (Mr. Marshall) took a little chip out of it
Hinweis: "... Mr. Marshall actually bit down on it. You can see the molar marks, his bite mark on it as well a little chip taken out of the upper left hand corner for assaying, or testing the purity of the gold." (Z. 11–13)

4. ... soft.
Hinweis: "Mr. Marshall knew he found gold because the metal was soft." (Z. 14)

5. ... from stories about it.
Hinweis: "People in the big eastern cities of New York and Boston heard only rumors about gold in California." (Z. 18–20)

6. ... often had wrong expectations.
   Hinweis: "You didn't really have to work for it, as far as they knew. You just had to lean over and pick it up and you were rich." (Z. 24/25)

7. ... had a very difficult life.
   Hinweis: "His wife tried to make a living by sewing and by borrowing money from the financiers against her husband's future profits. But it was not any easier for her than it was for her husband 3,000 miles away in California." (Z. 31–34)

8. ... did not make a lot of money.
   Hinweis: "Most people who traveled to California to find gold were like Van Valen – they did not get rich." (Z. 35–37)

9. ... joined the USA.
   Hinweis: "The Gold Rush [...] made the East Coast want California to become part of the United States." (Z. 39–41); "In 1850, California became the country's 31st state." (Z. 42)
   Im Text kommt zwar auch der Satz "The Gold Rush really put California on the map." (Z. 39) vor. Das ist aber nicht wörtlich, sondern im übertragenen Sinn gemeint: Die Wendung „to put something on the map" bedeutet so viel wie „to make something famous".

Listening Test 7: The Stolen Generations

1. ... 1970.
   Hinweis: "From the late nineteeth century to about 1970, various Australian governments took Aboriginal children – or children who had at least one Aboriginal parent – away from their families." (Z. 5–7)

2. ... adopt ...
   Hinweis: "Their aim was to make them adopt white culture." (Z. 7/8)

3. ... wipe out the Aboriginal way of life.
   Hinweis: "Well, basically, the governments were trying to get rid of Aboriginal peoples and their traditions. They thought that if Aboriginal children were forced to adopt white culture, the Aboriginal way of life would soon die out." (Z. 10–13)

4. ... far away from their parents.
   Hinweis: "The children were separated from their parents – their families – and often taken thousands of miles away, so they would never see each other again." (Z. 19–21)

5. ... take new names and speak English.
   Hinweis: "Most were given 'white' names and the only language they were allowed to use was English ..." (Z. 24/25)

6. ... were not looked after well.
   Hinweis: "In the homes, children were badly treated and often left cold and hungry." (Z. 29/30)

7. ... Sorry ...
   Hinweis: "One of its suggestions was to have an annual National Sorry Day for all Australians to remember this part of their country's history ..." (Z. 36–38)

8. ▶ lit the Olympic fire
   ▶ won a gold medal
   ▶ (ran around the track and) carried both the Aboriginal and the Australian flag
   Hinweis: "In 2000, during the Olympic Games in Sydney, an Aboriginal runner was chosen to light the Olympic fire. After winning a gold medal, she ran around the track carrying both the Aboriginal flag and the Australian one – a powerful symbol of reconciliation." (Z. 39–42)
   Du musst nur zwei der drei Aspekte nennen.

9. ... a lot of Aboriginal children are still taken away from their parents.
   Hinweis: "... apparently, the number of children who are taken away from their parents is still much higher for Aboriginal people than for white people. Even today, governments seem to spend a lot more money on putting Aboriginal children into state-run homes than on helping them to stay with their parents." (Z. 47–51)

Listening Test 8: Couchsurfing or Wilderness?

1. Olivia **F**
   Hinweis: "I don't want to be seen as a tourist" (Z. 11); „... explore places far away from the typical tourist paths." (Z. 13/14)

2. Hailey **C**
   Hinweis: "I wouldn't like to go couchsurfing. I think it's dangerous to stay at the house of someone you don't know." (Z. 15/16)

3. Carter **A**
   Hinweis: "I love hiking and fishing and being outside 24/7..." (Z. 21/22)

4. Josh **B**
   Hinweis: "Camping is great, isn't it?" (Z. 25); "I like sleeping in the comfy bed of the mobile home ..." (Z. 26/27)

5. Sara **G**
   Hinweis: "Staying at a hotel's just too expensive for a family of six and a dog ..." (Z. 31/32)

Listening Test 9: Inventing Elliot

1. ... lay in his bed.
   Hinweis: "He had just got into bed ..." (Z. 1)

2. ... talked about his father.
   Hinweis: "You've got to be patient with him, Elliot. He's ill." (Z. 4); "[Elliot] looked away from her, remembering the night his dad didn't come home." (Z. 10)

3. ... sad.
   Hinweis: "You've got to be patient with him, Elliot." (Z. 4); "'I just wish –' [...] 'You just wish it was like it was before. I know ...'" (Z. 7/8)

4. ... missed him a lot.
   Hinweis: "That hadn't been so great: it meant he often skipped meals at home. Elliot missed the three of them eating together ..." (Z. 12/13)

5. … unfamiliar voices under his bedroom.
   Hinweis: "He heard the door open, unfamiliar voices, the door close again, chairs scraping across the kitchen floor under his bedroom." (Z. 17/18)

6. … two police officers.
   Hinweis: "Two police uniforms: a man and a woman." (Z. 28)

7. … to get dressed.
   Hinweis: "Can you go and get dressed?" (Z. 34)

8. … walking back to his car.
   Hinweis: "His dad had been attacked walking back to his car." (Z. 44)

9. … severe.
   Hinweis: „fractured his skull, broken his ribs, ruptured his spleen." (Z. 46/47); "Visiting his dad in hospital; seeing his face swollen up like a puffball, tubes coming out of his nose, wrists and chest; watching him unable to move, hardly able to speak." (Z. 51–53)

10. … had come home.
    Hinweis: "… that was three years ago. The bones had mended. His dad had come home." (Z. 55)

Listening Test 10: Sandringham

1. … one of Queen Victoria's children.
   Hinweis: "The Royal Family have owned the house since 1862, when Queen Victoria bought it for her son." (Z. 5/6)

2. … 1977.
   Hinweis: "… it wasn't until 1977 that people were allowed into a small part of the house." (Z. 10/11)

3. … a large part of the countryside near it.
   Hinweis: "… there is Sandringham Estate, the land surrounding the house, which is also owned by the Royal Family. It includes part of the coast as well as many villages and farms." (Z. 13–15)

4. … can enjoy the gardens before arriving at the house.
   Hinweis: "The gardens are very big and colourful, and you have to walk a long way through them to get to the house." (Z. 17/18)

5. … get to see only a part of the house.
   Hinweis: "You don't see many rooms in the house … " (Z. 21); "… it wasn't until 1977 that people were allowed into a small part of the house." (Z. 10/11)

6. … made (much) longer …
   Hinweis: "There are even ones which were specially built for the Royal Family – for example, one made much longer so that it could take all their suitcases to the train station …" (Z. 27–29)

7. … the train …
   Hinweis: "… Queen Elizabeth II used to sit with normal passengers in a first-class coach on the train when she traveled back to London!" (Z. 30–32)

8. … on Christmas Day.
   Hinweis: "… Christmas Day always includes a walk to the church on the estate …" (Z. 34)

9. … does annoying things.
   Hinweis: "No one knows what the ghost looks like but it throws books off shelves and alters the time on clocks." (Z. 38/39)

Listening Test 11: The Super Bowl

1. … the most important American football organisation until 1960.
   Hinweis: "Well, for a long time the most important organisation for American football in the USA was the National Football League, – the NFL. But in 1960 a group of businessmen became dissatisfied with the organisation, so they started another one …" (Z. 8–11)

2. (constant) fights over (who got) the best players
   or: (had) fought over (who attracted) the most fans
   or: the rivalry between the two leagues
   Hinweis: "… there were constant fights over who got the best players, and of course also over who attracted the most fans. So in 1966, the two leagues

eventually gave up their rivalry and decided to merge into one common league." (Z. 13–16)

3. ... a kid's toy.
   Hinweis: "... a club owner jokingly named the final the 'Super Bowl' after one of his children's toys, the 'Super Ball'." (Z. 21/22)

4. (the) last game each college team played in their league
   or: new stadium at Yale University / Yale Bowl / shape of stadium
   or: many stadiums and competitions
   Hinweis: "In American football, the term 'bowl' was traditionally used for the last game each college team played in their league. Also, when a new stadium was built at Yale University in 1913, it was called the 'Yale Bowl' because of its shape. After that, many other stadiums and competitions included the word 'bowl'." (Z. 26–30)

5. ... 1967.
   Hinweis: "So when did the first Super Bowl game take place? 1966 or 1967? – In 1967 ..." (Z. 31/32)

6. ... not all the seats were sold.
   Hinweis: "They couldn't sell all the tickets!" (Z. 33)

7. ... the first Sunday in February.
   Hinweis: "It's always on the first Sunday in February ..." (Z. 44)

8. stadium with at least 70,000 seats
   or: good infrastructure
   Hinweis: "... they must have a stadium with at least 70,000 seats and of course a good infrastructure." (Z. 45/46)

9. ... the most watched sporting event in the USA.
   Hinweis: "The Super Bowl is usually the most watched sporting event in the USA ..." (Z. 49/50)

Listening Test 12: Sundae Girl

1. … Parents' Night at school.
   ✎ *Hinweis: "Nobody likes Parents' Night, do they? […] Your parents discover that […] you've only handed in one maths homework …" (Z. 1–3); "I'm not worried that my family will find out the truth about school – I'm more anxious that school will find out the truth about my family." (Z. 7/8)*

2. … ashamed of her family.
   ✎ *Hinweis: : "… I'm more anxious that school will find out the truth about my family. And now they are here for Parents' Night – all of them. Nightmare." (Z. 7–9)*

3. … a hairdresser.
   ✎ *Hinweis: "'You're a hairdresser, Mum,' I mumble." (Z. 19)*

4. … are separated.
   ✎ *Hinweis: "Mum and Dad are no longer together …" (Z. 26)*

5. … is in Jude's English class.
   ✎ *Hinweis: "… Kevin Carter from my English class is sipping a cup of tea." (Z. 34)*

6. … an Elvis impersonator.
   ✎ *Hinweis: "… Dad is an Elvis impersonator." (Z. 43)*

7. … pretty.
   ✎ *Hinweis: "Kristina Kowalski is hot!" (Z. 51)*

8. … a tie.
   ✎ *Hinweis: "Grandad is wearing his yellow tartan waistcoat with the Marilyn Monroe tie …" (Z. 54/55)*

9. … unusual.
   ✎ *Hinweis: "Grandad is wearing his yellow tartan waistcoat with the Marilyn Monroe tie, and Gran is knitting as she waits." (Z. 54/55); "Unreal! I wonder what poor kid has got grandparents like that?" (Z. 58/59)*

10. … pretends she is not related to them.
    ✎ *Hinweis: "'Actually,' I tell him, 'They're Kristina Kowalski's mum and dad.'" (Z. 62)*

Listening Test 13: Mary Robinson

1. … inspiring Irish personalities.
   Hinweis: "… in each of our episodes, young people present their personal heroes, people they find particularly inspiring." (Z. 2/3)

2. … was the first female president of Ireland.
   Hinweis: "Mary Robinson was president of Ireland between 1990 and 1997, and she was also the first woman to hold that office." (Z. 8/9)

3. … for the rights of women, gay and lesbian people.
   Hinweis: "… she fought for the rights of women to get access to the contraceptive pill and demanded that same-sex relationships should no longer be regarded as a crime." (Z. 15–18)

4. ▶ (her) capacity to build bridges
   ▶ (her) willingness to stand up for marginalised groups
   Hinweis: "For one thing, her capacity to build bridges. […] And secondly, her willingness to stand up for marginalised groups." (Z. 26–30)

5. … *Everybody Matters.*
   Hinweis: "Her memoir is entitled Everybody Matters … *" (Z. 34/35)*

6. … is regarded as a moral authority.
   Hinweis: "… she is a member of the so-called 'Elders'. This is a group founded by Nelson Mandela which consists of leaders who are known for their wisdom and strong moral convictions." (Z. 39–41)

7. … climate change and human rights are closely linked.
   Hinweis: "… for her, climate change also concerns human rights: If the weather becomes more extreme, people will lose their homes and often their lives, and although rich countries produce the most greenhouse gas emissions, it is the poor that suffer the worst from changing weather conditions." (Z. 44–48)

Listening Test 14: New Zealand Tips

1. … are used for tourism.
   Hinweis: "… they're used for tourism and for activities such as rafting, canoeing or bungy jumping." (Z. 10/11)

2. … originated in New Zealand.
   Hinweis: "Bungy jumping was invented … you may have guessed it … in New Zealand!" (Z. 12/13)

3. hotspot for kayaking and rafting
   or: Māori term for "flowing river"
   or: longest river in New Zealand
   Hinweis: "… I prefer kayaking and rafting. One of my favourite places is Waikato River, which is a hotspot for these activities. […] – Waikato is not an English name, is it? – No, it's not. It's a Māori term, meaning 'flowing river'. It's the longest river in New Zealand." (Z. 16–21)

4. … winter sports.
   Hinweis: "I also really like the winter months from June to August when the mountains are covered in snow and you can go skiing or snowboarding." (Z. 24–26)

5. … take place throughout the country.
   Hinweis: "… there are guided tours all over the country." (Z. 35/36)

6. … marvel at the beautiful surroundings.
   Hinweis: "The view is awesome, there are enormous stone and rock formations" (Z. 43/44)

7. … sports and outdoor activities.
   Hinweis: Bei dieser Aufgabe wird danach gefragt, wovon die Podcastfolge überwiegend handelt. Wahrscheinlich kannst du die Frage bereits durch den Gesamteindruck des Gehörten beantworten; wenn du dir unsicher bist, solltest du nach dem Ausschlussprinzip vorgehen: Im Text wird zwar der Begriff Māori genannt, es geht aber nicht in erster Linie um kulturelle Stätten der Māori. Das Thema Ökotourismus wird gar nicht angesprochen – diese Möglichkeit scheidet also ebenfalls aus. Stattdessen ist viel von Sport und Aktivitäten im Freien die Rede – die dritte Auswahlmöglichkeit ist also richtig.

▶ Lösungen zum Leseverstehen

Allgemeiner Hinweis: In diesem Kapitel kannst du dein Leseverstehen trainieren. Da du hier die Möglichkeit hast, den Text noch einmal durchzulesen, werden manchmal genauere Details abgefragt als in den Aufgaben zum Hörverstehen. Du solltest die Texte also besonders aufmerksam lesen.

Reading Test 1: The Kiwi – New Zealand's Iconic Bird

Aufgabe 1

Hinweis: Bei dieser Aufgabe musst du entscheiden, ob bestimmte Aussagen über den Text richtig oder falsch sind, und das entsprechende Kästchen abhaken. Außerdem sollst du anhand einer Textstelle belegen, warum du dich für „true" oder „false" entschieden hast. Lies dir als erstes den ganzen Text einmal durch. Danach siehst du dir die Aussagen an. Um zu entscheiden, ob eine Aussage richtig oder falsch ist, musst du zunächst herausfinden, an welcher Stelle im Text die passende Information zu finden ist. Dazu solltest du den Text noch einmal überfliegen und darauf achten, ob du bestimmte Schlüsselwörter oder Synonyme zu den Begriffen aus der Aussage im Text wiederfindest. Verlasse dich aber nie „blind" auf ein Schlüsselwort, sondern lies dir die entsprechende Textstelle ganz genau durch, beziehe auch den Textzusammenhang mit ein und vergleiche noch einmal genau, wie die Textstelle und die Aussage formuliert sind.
Beachte, dass es bei diesem Aufgabenformat keine teilweise richtigen Antworten gibt. In der Prüfung bekommst du also entweder zwei Punkte, wenn sowohl dein Häkchen als auch dein Textbeleg richtig sind, oder null Punkte, wenn eines von beiden (oder beide) falsch sind.

a) false
Evidence: the kiwi [...] hides in self-dug small holes during the day. That is why you hardly ever see it in the wilderness. / it is difficult to encounter a bird in the wild
Hinweis: Z. 15–19; Z. 68/69

b) true
Evidence: Kiwis are monogamous – they stay with the same partner their whole life.
Hinweis: Z. 21/22

c) true
Evidence: They wore "kahu kiwi", cloaks made from its feathers.
Hinweis: Z. 25/26

d) false
Evidence: Predators such as cats [...] had not existed in New Zealand before
Hinweis: Z. 32–34

e) false
Evidence: They also use this expression themselves because they are proud of their unique country
Hinweis: Z. 62–64

f) true
Evidence: the star is always the kiwi
Hinweis: Z. 73

g) false
Evidence: there are less than 70,000 kiwis left and their number is falling continuously
Hinweis: Z. 79–81

Aufgabe 2

Hinweis: Bei dieser Zuordnungsaufgabe musst du zu jeder Überschrift den zugehörigen Abschnitt im Text finden.

1. Origin of the name "kiwi" **D**
   Hinweis: In Absatz D werden zwei Theorien aufgeführt, wie der Kiwi zu seinem Namen kam. Das Schlüsselwort „name" taucht sowohl in der Überschrift als auch im Textabschnitt (vgl. Z. 41) auf.

2. Places to see kiwis **F**
   Hinweis: Zu Überschrift 2 passt die Formulierung „opportunities to see a kiwi" (Z. 67) aus Textabschnitt F.

3. An animal in danger **C**
   Hinweis: Das Wort „danger" aus der Überschrift und das Synonym „threat" tauchen auch in Textabschnitt C auf (vgl. Z. 29 und Z. 35). In diesem Abschnitt wird ausgeführt, wodurch der Kiwi bedroht wird.

4. Becoming a national icon **E**
   *Hinweis: Bei dieser Überschrift geht es darum, wie der Kiwi zu einem nationalen Symbol für Neuseeland wurde. In Textabschnitt E wird ausgeführt, wie Name und Bild des Kiwi-Vogels weltweit bekannt wurden, sodass der Begriff „Kiwi" heute sogar als Bezeichnung für die Einwohner*innen Neuseelands verwendet wird.*

5. A slightly different national animal **A**
   Hinweis: Diese Überschrift ist bereits vorgegeben.

6. Efforts to save the kiwi **G**
   Hinweis: In Textabschnitt G wird zunächst erwähnt, dass die Zahl der Kiwis immer weiter sinkt. Anschließend ist von „projects in order to rescue the bird from extinction" (Z. 82/83) die Rede – das entspricht den „[e]fforts to save the kiwi" aus Überschrift 6.

7. Appearance and typical behaviour **B**
   Hinweis: In Textabschnitt B wird zunächst das Aussehen des Kiwis beschrieben und dann werden einige typische Verhaltensweisen genannt (z. B. dass Kiwis nachtaktiv sind und sich zum Schlafen Löcher graben, sich von Würmern, Obst und Insekten ernähren; dass sich Paare finden, die ein Leben lang zusammenbleiben).

Aufgabe 3

Hinweis: Bei dieser Aufgabe sollst du Fragen beantworten – deine Antworten müssen aber nicht unbedingt in vollständigen Sätzen formuliert sein.

a) ▶ predators that had not existed in New Zealand before / new species that settlers had brought with them / cats, dogs, weasels and possums
   ▶ loss of living space / humans who destroy the living space of the kiwi
   Hinweis: Du findest die relevanten Informationen in den Zeilen 32–39.

b) ▶ named after (shrill) call of male kiwi ("kiwii-kiwii")
▶ named after the Polynesian kivi (a bird that looks similar to the kiwi)
Hinweis: Die beiden Theorien sind in Abschnitt D (Z. 40–46) zu finden.

c) (one of the) 13 national parks (run by the DOC)
or: National Kiwi Centre in Hokitika
Hinweis: Die gesuchte Information verbirgt sich in Abschnitt F (Z. 69–71 und Z. 74/75).

Aufgabe 4

Hinweis: Bei dieser Aufgabe ist immer nur eine Wahlmöglichkeit zutreffend. Vergleiche ganz genau mit dem Text und kreuze nur die Möglichkeit an, für die du eine oder mehrere Textstellen als „Beweis(e)" finden kannst. Bei Teilaufgabe a) musst du den Textbeleg nicht extra angeben; bei b) und c) wird jedoch von dir verlangt, die entsprechende Stelle zu zitieren.

a) … lion.
Hinweis: In Abschnitt A wird erwähnt, dass das Vereinigte Königreich den „König des Dschungels", den Löwen, als Nationaltier hat (vgl. Z. 2–4).

b) … in the 19th century.
Evidence: Around the middle of the 19th century, pictures of the kiwi appeared on regimental badges of the New Zealand army.
Hinweis: Z. 47–50

c) … in Britain and America.
Evidence: an Australian boot polish called "Kiwi" was […] sold in the US and the United Kingdom
Hinweis: Z. 54–57

Aufgabe 5

Hinweis: Bei dieser Zusatzaufgabe sollst du einen Steckbrief über den Kiwi-Vogel mit den passenden Informationen aus dem Text ergänzen.

The Kiwi

Living space: forests in New Zealand

Size: about the size of a domestic chicken

Food: worms, centipedes, fruits, insects

Sleeping place: self-dug holes

What is special about it: it can't fly,

but its sense of smell is very good

Reading Test 2: Young Refugees Learn about U.S. on the Soccer Field

Aufgabe 1

a) ... Thailand.
Evidence: Win was born in Thailand
Hinweis: Z. 6

b) false
Evidence: Win and his ten family members share two apartments.
Hinweis: Z. 14/15

c)
- (he has a) chance to get a better education
- (he gets to play) soccer without worrying about gunshots / (he) does not have to worry about gunshots

Hinweis: Win liebt an seiner neuen Heimat, dass er eine Chance auf eine gute Bildung bekommt und Fußball spielen kann, ohne sich über Schüsse (bzw. Krieg und Gewalt im Allgemeinen) Sorgen machen zu müssen (vgl. Z. 20–23).

d) ... can learn more than just soccer rules.
Evidence: The soccer club has helped him ... learn more about his new home. / His coaches have taught his family about life in the United States.
Hinweis: Z. 24–27

e)
- (she can) teach kids things that their parents can't
- (she can) do something good for the refugees / help the refugees
- can relate to the refugees' experiences (of not being accepted/of being treated differently)

Hinweis: Alondra Ruiz empfindet die Arbeit für den Fußballverein als bereichernd. Sie erkennt sich selbst in den Kindern wieder und kann ihre eigenen Erfahrungen nutzen, um ihnen den Einstieg in das neue Leben zu erleichtern. Dabei hat sie das Gefühl, etwas Gutes und Sinnvolles zu tun. Es reicht, wenn du zwei der drei oben genannten Aspekte angibst.

f) false
Evidence: her husband has permission to work in the U.S.
Hinweis: Z. 50/51

g) true

Evidence: Arizona … is among the top 10 resettling states in the U.S.

Hinweis: Um diese Frage zu beantworten, hilft dir evtl. auch die Fußnote mit der Erklärung zum Wort „resettlement program". Arizona gehört zu den „top 10 resettling states", unternimmt also mehr, um geflüchtete Menschen aufzunehmen und willkommenzuheißen als viele andere US Staaten (vgl. Z. 52–54).

h)
- (they) have to learn English / a new language
- (they) have to get used to the new environment
- (they) are treated differently / (they) are not accepted

Hinweis: Du findest an mehreren Stellen Informationen zu den Schwierigkeiten, mit denen Geflüchtete besonders zu Beginn zu kämpfen haben: Sie kommen in eine neue Umgebung, die sich von der gewohnten unterscheidet (vgl. Z. 27–30), sie müssen eine neue Sprache lernen (vgl. Z. 60–65) und sind Diskriminierung ausgesetzt bzw. haben das Gefühl, nicht akzeptiert zu werden (vgl. Z. 44–47). Auch hier reicht es wieder, wenn du zwei Aspekte nennst.

Aufgabe 2

Hinweis: Bei dieser Aufgabe sollst du zu den Personen bzw. dem Fußballverein jeweils eine passende Aussage finden. Gehe den Text der Reihe nach für jede Person bzw. den Verein durch und lies noch einmal, was zu ihm bzw. ihr gesagt wird. Du solltest deine Zuordnung mit einer oder mehreren Textstellen „beweisen" können, auch wenn die Aufgabe nicht von dir verlangt, dass du diese Textstellen angibst. Manchmal passen evtl. mehrere Zuordnungen, dann musst du im Ausschlussverfahren vorgehen.

❶ Win La Bar **C**

Hinweis: Am Ende des zweiten Absatzes äußert sich Win über die Chancen, die er in seiner neuen Heimat hat (vgl. Z. 20–23). Vielleicht wünscht er sich auch, amerikanischer Staatsbürger zu werden, dies kann man aber nicht am Text belegen. Aussage D passt daher nicht zu ihm.

❷ North Phoenix Christian Soccer Club **F**

Hinweis: Die Angebote des Fußballclubs, der den Kindern neben Fußballtraining auch Hilfe bei der Orientierung in der neuen Umgebung bietet (vgl. Z. 24–27), kann man als eine Art Integrationsprogramm ansehen. Mit dem schulischen Erfolg der Kinder hat dies nicht unbedingt etwas zu tun, daher passt Aussage A nicht.

❸ Alondra Ruiz **D**

Hinweis: In Zeile 51 erfährt man, dass Alondra Ruiz illegal in den USA lebt – der Wunsch, amerikanische Staatsbürgerin zu werden und somit legal in dem Land leben zu dürfen, passt daher am ehesten zu ihr.

❹ Zara Doukoum **B**

Hinweis: Hier musst du im Ausschlussverfahren vorgehen. Zu Zara passt sowohl Aussage B als auch C. Aussage C passt auch zu Win, Aussage B kann aber nur von Zara kommen, die selbst schon bald die Schule beenden wird (vgl. Z. 71/72) und darüber spricht, wie schwierig es am Anfang war (vgl. Z. 60–65).

Reading Test 3: The History of Halloween

Aufgabe 1

a) true
Evidence: our modern holiday "Halloween" goes back to the old Gaelic festival of "Samhain"
Hinweis: Z. 1–3

b) ... for about 24 hours.
Evidence: It was celebrated from sunset on October 31st to sunset on November 1st.
Hinweis: Die Feierlichkeiten gingen vom Sonnenuntergang am 31. Oktober bis zum Sonnenuntergang am 1. November, d. h., sie dauerten insgesamt nur ca. 24 Stunden und nicht etwa zwei ganze Tage oder mehrere Monate (vgl. Z. 6–8).

c)
- (they lit) bonfires
- (they held) special feasts and meals
- (they made) offerings to the (old) gods and "aos sí"

Hinweis: Für das Samhain-Fest wurden große Feuer entzündet, besonderes Essen zubereitet und den Göttern und übernatürlichen Wesen Opfer dargebracht (vgl. Z. 14–20). Du musst nur zwei der drei Aspekte nennen.

d) ... supernatural beings.
Evidence: the "aos sí", a mystical and supernatural race comparable to fairies or elves
Hinweis: Z. 17–19

e) true
Evidence: In those costumes they sometimes went from house to house and asked for blessings and small gifts.
Hinweis: Z. 38–41

Aufgabe 2

Hinweis: Hier musst du die Abschnitte des Textes ordnen. Ein Text ist oft so aufgebaut, dass am Anfang etwas Allgemeines erklärt und danach Beispiele genannt oder Vergleiche gezogen werden. Wörter wie z. B. „thus" oder „for example" zeigen an, dass etwas vorher bereits Genanntes nun näher ausgeführt wird; Ausdrücke wie „however" oder „by contrast" leiten häufig einen Vergleich ein. Wörter wie diese können dir also helfen, die logische Reihenfolge der Textabschnitte zu erkennen.

❶ Textabschnitt C ist vorgegeben.

❷ Textabschnitt A
Hinweis: Im vorigen Textabschnitt (C) wurde ausgeführt, dass die katholische Kirche ihre eigenen Feiertage so legte, dass sie zeitlich mit Festivitäten aus anderen Religionen zusammenfielen – als Beispiele wurden Ostern und Weihnachten genannt, die jeweils auf römische bzw. jüdische Festtage gelegt wurden. In Abschnitt A wird nun ein weiteres Beispiel erwähnt, nämlich die Verlagerung des katholischen Feiertags Allerheiligen auf das Datum des keltischen Samhain-Festes.

❸ Textabschnitt D
Hinweis: Im vorigen Abschnitt (A) ging es um das Allerheiligenfest und es wurde erwähnt, dass der Vorabend „All Hallow's Eve" genannt wurde. Die Formulierung „this phrase" in Abschnitt D bezieht sich direkt darauf zurück.

❹ Textabschnitt B
Hinweis: In Abschnitt D wurde ausgeführt, dass Halloween und Allerheiligen auf das keltische Samhain-Fest zurückgehen. Abschnitt B schließt sich inhaltlich an, da hier erwähnt wird, dass sich heute nur noch wenige Menschen des keltischen Ursprungs von Halloween bewusst sind.

Reading Test 4: Getting to Know Canada

Aufgabe 1

a) ... an informative text that might be part of an online travel guide about Canada.

✎ *Hinweis: Einige Wahlmöglichkeiten kannst du schon anhand des Layouts des Textes ausschließen. Die Seite sieht nicht aus wie ein Flyer bzw. Prospekt (= „leaflet"), sondern es handelt sich eindeutig um eine Website. Inhaltlich passt „about the history of Canada" (zweite Wahlmöglichkeit) nicht zum Text, in dem es nur ganz am Rande um Geschichte geht. Es bleibt also nur das letzte Satzende übrig. In einem Online-Reiseführer (= „online travel guide") könnte es eine solche allgemeine Einführung zu Kanada geben.*

b) false

Evidence: It consists of ten provinces and three territories.

✎ *Hinweis: Z. 2/3*

c) ... a member of the British royal family.

Evidence: Prince Edward Island, named after Queen Victoria's father

✎ *Hinweis: Prince Edward Island ist nach dem Vater von Königin Victoria (vgl. Z. 4) benannt.*

d) true

Evidence: about 31,000 people live there, 85 % of whom are indigenous

✎ *Hinweis: Circa „85 %", also eine deutliche Mehrheit, der Einwohner von Nunavut gehören einer der ursprünglichen Bevölkerungsgruppen von Kanada an (vgl. Z. 11/12).*

e)
- very cold / coldest territory
- no roads that connect communities with each other and the rest of Canada / difficult to get from one community to another / far away from the rest of the country

✎ *Hinweis: Du solltest hier auf die schwierigen Bedingungen im Norden Kanadas eingehen. Es ist dort sehr kalt und das Klima sorgt auch dafür, dass man nicht die gleichen Möglichkeiten hat sich fortzubewegen wie im Rest des Landes. Diese Informationen stehen in den Zeilen 10–16.*

f) … French.
Hinweis: Französisch ist die Amtssprache von Quebec, d. h., man kann davon ausgehen, dass ein Großteil der Bevölkerung Französisch spricht. Viele Menschen in Quebec beherrschen zwar auch das Englische (vgl. Z. 21/22), sprechen es aber nicht ausschließlich – die zweite Möglichkeit („English only") scheidet daher aus. Eine indigene Sprache wird nirgends im Text erwähnt – diese Option ist daher ebenfalls falsch.

g) … protect plants and animals.
Hinweis: "More than a century ago, in 1885, when people realised that it was necessary to protect plants and animals, the history of Canada's national parks started …" (Z. 23/24)

h) … you should go by boat.
Hinweis: "Thrill-seeking visitors, however, might want to go on a cruise that travels past the American and Bridal Veil Falls to get as close to the Horseshoe Falls as possible." (Z. 36–39)

Aufgabe 2

Hinweis: Nimm dir der Reihe nach die fünf geographischen Bezeichnungen vor und überfliege den Text mehrmals. Markiere alle Textstellen farbig, in denen die Begriffe auftauchen. Wenn du dir diese Stellen genauer ansiehst und die Informationen mit der Landkarte vergleichst, kannst du die Städte, Regionen etc. sicher schnell auf der Karte finden.

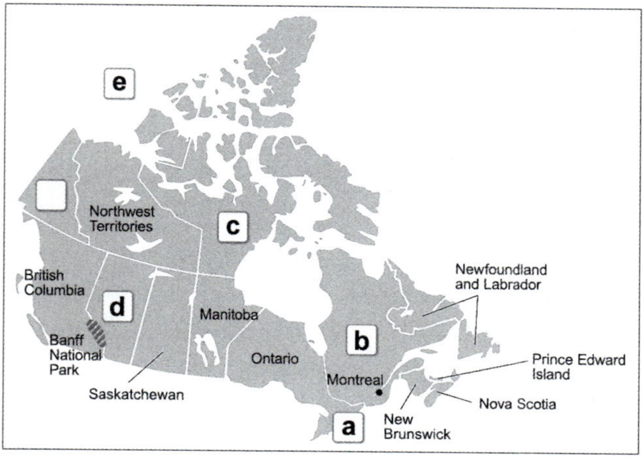

✎ *Hinweis:*

zu a: Die Niagarafälle liegen zum Teil in Ontario/Kanada, zum Teil auf US-amerikanischem Staatsgebiet (vgl. Z. 30/31, 39–42). Zu a) passt daher das Feld auf der Karte, das zur Hälfte in Ontario und zur anderen Hälfte in den USA liegt.

zu b: Das Stichwort „Quebec" (Z. 20) fällt in Abschnitt C. In dieser französischsprachigen Provinz Kanadas liegt auch die Stadt „Montreal" (Z. 22), die auch in der Karte eingezeichnet ist.

zu c: Im Text erfährst du, dass Nunavut „the largest territory" (Z. 4/5) in Kanada ist, und dass diese Region sehr weit im Norden liegt (vgl. Z. 5).

zu d: In der Provinz Alberta (Z. 25) befindet sich der Banff National Park, den du auch in der Karte siehst.

zu e: Aus dem Text weißt du, dass der arktische Ozean im Norden an Kanada grenzt (vgl. Z. 6/7).

Aufgabe 3

✎ *Hinweis: Bei dieser Aufgabe musst du für jeden Textabschnitt eine passende Überschrift auswählen. Zwei Überschriften passen nicht zum Text. Lies die möglichen Überschriften ganz genau und vergleiche sie mit den Absätzen im Text. Sei besonders vorsichtig bei Überschriften, die ähnlich klingen. Manchmal unterscheiden sie sich nur in einem Detail. Dann musst du prüfen, ob dieses Detail wirklich zum Text passt.*

1. All the languages spoken in Canada **–**
   ✎ *Hinweis: Vorsicht, lass dich hier nicht in die Irre führen. Man könnte zwar denken, dass diese Überschrift zu Absatz C passt, hier geht es aber speziell um Kanadas Amtssprachen (= „official languages", vgl. Überschrift 5), nicht um „all the languages".*

2. How to visit Niagara Falls **E**
   ✎ *Hinweis: Im letzten Abschnitt des Textes (E) wird beschrieben, welche Möglichkeiten es gibt, die Niagarafälle zu erleben.*

3. Geographical facts and background information **A**
   ✎ *Hinweis: Der erste Textabschnitt (A) gibt allgemeine Informationen zu Kanada, u. a. zur Geographie.*

4. Life in the far north **B**
Hinweis: In Abschnitt B geht es um Nunavut, welches im äußersten Norden des Landes liegt.

5. Canada's official languages **C**
Hinweis: Diese Überschrift passt zu Abschnitt C.

6. Winter in Nunavut **–**
Hinweis: In Abschnitt B geht es zwar um Nunavut – diese Überschrift ist aber nicht treffend, denn der Text informiert nicht nur über den Winter dort, sondern allgemein über die Lebensbedingungen in diesem Teil Kanadas.

7. National parks in Canada **D**
Hinweis: Abschnitt D beschäftigt sich mit den kanadischen Nationalparks.

Reading Test 5: Volunteering in Australia

1. … he was too young to take part in the volunteer programme alone.
Evidence: At first his age was a problem as Conservation Volunteers Australia (CVA) … requires international volunteers to be over the age of 18.
Hinweis: Z. 14–19

2. false
Evidence: Many of them … decide to do voluntary work for a few weeks.
Hinweis: Z. 29–32

3. ▶ (they) want to do something useful
▶ (they) want to help with conservation
▶ (they want to earn the right to) travel in the country
▶ (they want to) experience something new
Hinweis: Hier sind zwei verschiedene Motive zu nennen. Zum einen ist der Aspekt, helfen zu wollen und etwas für den Umweltschutz zu tun, relevant (vgl. z. B. Z. 29–36). Zum anderen spielt auch der Wunsch, etwas Neues / ein Abenteuer erleben und das Land kennenlernen zu wollen, eine Rolle: „looking for a new experience" (Z. 22/23); „travel in the country" (Z. 35). Du kannst auch aus den Erfahrungsberichten im letzten Absatz Motive für eine Reise nach Australien und die Freiwilligenarbeit ableiten.

4. true
   Evidence: There are all sorts of projects in Australia in need of volunteers who are willing to get their hands dirty for a while.
   ✎ *Hinweis: Z. 37–39*

5. ▶ collect rubbish
   ▶ plant trees
   ▶ remove plants that do not naturally belong to the Australian landscape
   ▶ restore the living space of threatened species
   ▶ construct/maintain walking trails
   ▶ build fences
   ▶ assist in research programmes
   ▶ set up cameras (to monitor endangered species)
   ✎ *Hinweis: Hier werden sehr viele verschiedene Aktivitäten im Text genannt (vgl. Z. 44–56) – es reicht aber, wenn du zwei angibst.*

6. false
   Evidence: Some of these volunteers are international travellers, but Australia is also known as a nation of volunteers
   ✎ *Hinweis: Z. 60–63*

7. … has changed them in a positive way.
   Evidence: I've grown as a person
   ✎ *Hinweis: Z. 87/88*

Reading Test 6: "We May Be 'Born Free', but …"

Aufgabe 1

1. … young South Africans born after the end of apartheid.
   Evidence: They are the first generation … who no longer experienced the system of racial segregation that had characterised South Africa for almost half a century.
   ✎ *Hinweis: Z. 6–13*

2. ... consider it normal to be living in a democratic society.
   Evidence: Young South Africans nowadays take many of the hard-won privileges for granted
   Hinweis: Z. 25–28

3. false
   Evidence: According to recent statistics, about 60 per cent of South Africans between the ages of 15 and 24 are out of work.
   Hinweis: Z. 36/37

4. ... can still be felt.
   Evidence: Even so many years after the end of apartheid, the old inequalities are still in place.
   Hinweis: Z. 45–47

5. false
   Evidence: Women are much more likely than men to be infected
   Hinweis: Z. 52/53

6. ▶ (they could) fight HIV/AIDS / improve medical treatment
   ▶ (they could) improve education
   ▶ (they could) create new jobs / fight unemployment
   Hinweis: Im Text werden mehrere Probleme der „born free"-Generation genannt (Arbeitslosigkeit, Gesundheit, Bildung, vgl. Z. 34–60), von denen du zwei für deine Antwort auswählen kannst.

7. ... stay in her country.
   Evidence: Has she ever considered leaving South Africa and moving to another country? – "I knew you would ask that. But no never."
   Hinweis: Z. 61–64

8. true
   Evidence: There are so many creative people, people who want to change things. We may be "born free", but there's still a lot for us to do in this society.
   Hinweis: Z. 66–69

9. true
   Evidence: people with British or Dutch roots enjoyed a lot of privileges
   Hinweis: vgl. Infokasten „What is Apartheid?"

10. ▶ (they) were not allowed to vote
▶ (they) were forced to live in particular areas / homelands
▶ (they) were not allowed to use the same facilities as white people
Hinweis: Für deine Antwort genügt es, wenn du zwei der drei Aspekte nennst. Die Informationen hierzu findest du im Infokasten „What is Apartheid?“.

Reading Test 7: School Life Abroad

Aufgabe 1

Hinweis: Bei diesem Aufgabenformat musst du wieder die verschiedenen Teile des Textes in die richtige Reihenfolge bringen. Lies dir erst alle Abschnitte durch und versuche, ungefähr zu verstehen, worum es jeweils geht. Suche Abschnitte, in denen ein ähnliches Thema behandelt wird. Dies erkennst du daran, dass Wörter wiederholt werden, oder dass Wörter aus derselben Wortfamilie auftauchen. Falls es mehrere Abschnitte zu einem Thema gibt, dann achte besonders auf Pronomen wie „it“, die sich auf Begriffe beziehen, die schon in den Sätzen <u>zuvor</u> genannt wurden. So kannst du dir nach und nach die richtige Reihenfolge der Abschnitte erschließen.

❶ Textabschnitt C
Hinweis: Dass Abschnitt C der erste Teil des Textes sein muss, erkennst du daran, dass auch Tanjas Nachname angegeben wird, während in den anderen Abschnitten immer nur ihr Vorname genannt wird. Inhaltlich geht es in dem Abschnitt um die erste Begegnung des Reporters mit Tanja, was ebenfalls gut an den Anfang der Reportage passt.

❷ Textabschnitt G
Hinweis: Im vorangegangenen Abschnitt (C) wurden bereits kurz Tanjas Sprachkenntnisse erwähnt („impressed by her English“) – dieser Aspekt wird in Abschnitt G wieder aufgegriffen („My English was rubbish“).

❸ Textabschnitt A
Hinweis: Am Ende von Abschnitt G wurde bereits erwähnt, dass Tanja bei einer Gastfamilie wohnt. Dieses Thema wird in Abschnitt A noch weiter ausgeführt, wenn Tanja über ihre Gasteltern und neuen „Schwestern“ spricht.

❹ Textabschnitt F

Hinweis: Am Ende von Abschnitt A wurde bereits erwähnt, dass Tanja eine Schule in Bristol besucht. Abschnitt F schließt sich hier nahtlos an, da darin beschrieben wird, wie sich Tanja dort zurechtfindet.

❺ Textabschnitt D

Hinweis: Im vorigen Abschnitt (F) wurde bereits die „school uniform" angesprochen, die auch in den Teilen B und D vorkommt. Zu der Aussage, dass Tanja die Uniform zuerst nicht mochte, dass sich dies aber geändert hat, passt der Beginn von D: „What she likes about it is …".

❻ Textabschnitt B

Hinweis: In Abschnitt B geht es weiter um die Schuluniform, außerdem wird ein neues Thema, die „registration" eingeführt. Eine Verknüpfung zwischen den Teilen B und D ist „polo shirt", das in D als Teil der Uniform aufgezählt wird, und auf das in Abschnitt B noch einmal genauer eingegangen wird.

❼ Textabschnitt E

Hinweis: In Abschnitt E wird das Thema aus Abschnitt B weiter ausgeführt – es wird sogar das Wort „registration" noch einmal wiederholt.

Reading Test 8: The Double Life of Cassiel Roadnight

Hinweis: Bei den Aufgaben zum Leseverstehen können dich in der MSA-Prüfung auch literarische Texte erwarten. In diesem Test kannst du überprüfen, wie du damit zurechtkommst.

1. … because he desperately needs something to eat.
   Evidence: I'd … walked in off the streets half-starved, because I had to.
   Hinweis: Z. 2–4

2. … not mentioned.
   Hinweis: Gordon ist der Name des Mannes, der den Erzähler befragt – diese Möglichkeit scheidet also aus. „Cassiel Roadnight" ist ebenfalls falsch, da der Erzähler an einer Stelle ausdrücklich sagt, dass dies nicht sein Name sei (vgl. Z. 31; lass dich nicht davon täuschen, dass er sich am Ende als Cassiel Roadnight ausgibt). Wie der Erzähler in Wirklichkeit heißt, erfahren wir nicht.

3. … think he might be a missing person.
   ✎ *Hinweis: Gordon und Ginny vermuten, dass es sich bei dem Erzähler um einen vermissten Jungen handelt, und behandeln ihn deshalb besonders umsichtig (vgl. Z. 20–27).*

4. ▶ (he) has (two) scars
   ▶ (he) has (five) piercings in his ears
   ▶ (he) has bad teeth / his teeth are bad
   ✎ *Hinweis: Über das Aussehen des Erzählers erfahren wir insgesamt drei Dinge, nämlich dass er Narben im Gesicht hat, dass er Ohrlöcher hat und dass seine Zähne schlecht sind (vgl. Z. 39–41). Es reicht, wenn du zwei Aspekte nennst.*

5. … a person he does not know.
   ✎ *Hinweis: Lass dich hier nicht in die Irre führen. Der Erzähler ist zwar im ersten Moment erstaunt, dass der Junge auf dem Bild genau wie er selbst aussieht. Nach einigen Momenten erkennt er aber einige Unterschiede, z. B. dass der Junge keine Narben, keine Ohrlöcher und schöne Zähne hat – das Bild zeigt also nicht ihn selbst (vgl. Z. 44). Der Erzähler scheint die Person auch nicht zu kennen, da er sich wundert, „how incredible it was to […] look exactly like a total stranger" (Z. 57/58).*

6. false
   Evidence: In the picture … I was happy and well fed and wholesome. In other words, it wasn't me. / And what did I have? Nobody. Nothing. I always wanted to be someone else.
   ✎ *Hinweis: Z. 42–44 und Z. 63/64*

7. … take on a new identity.
   ✎ *Hinweis: Der Erzähler beschließt am Ende, sich als Cassiel Roadnight, der Junge aus der Vermisstenanzeige, auszugeben.*

Reading Test 9: Boot Camps for Teenagers

1. … for the army.
   Hinweis: "The name was first used by the U.S. military for camps in which new soldiers were trained under extreme conditions." (Z. 8–11)

2. … break people's will.
   Evidence: The idea was to break a person down and rebuild them with the "correct" behaviour.
   Hinweis: Z. 19–21

3. ▶ deterrence / keep young people from committing crime / the idea that they could go to boot camps should scare youths
   ▶ reduce the number of prisoners
   ▶ lower (the) costs
   ▶ lower (the) rate of recidivism / prevent young people from returning to crime
   Hinweis: Hier wird nach den Zielen gefragt, die mit den Bootcamps für Jugendliche verfolgt wurden. Du findest die entsprechenden Informationen in den Zeilen 26–34 und kannst zwei Aspekte auswählen.

4. true
   Evidence: Teenagers have to stay at boot camp for 90 to 180 days.
   Hinweis: Z. 37/38

5. ▶ (they) can be sent by a judge
   ▶ (they) can be sent by their parents
   ▶ (they) can choose boot camp instead of a prison sentence
   Hinweis: Im Text werden insgesamt drei Möglichkeiten genannt, von denen du zwei in deiner Antwort nennen musst. Du findest sie in den Zeilen 38–44.

6. … there have been attempts to reform the system.
   Hinweis: "As a reaction to the criticism, many boot camps now also offer other activities: educational courses, therapy, and special programmes for drug addicts." (Z. 54–57)

7. … is more or less equal with boot camps and prisons.
   Hinweis: "The rate of recidivism for boot camps and prisons is about the same …" (Z. 64/65)

8. true
   Evidence: boot camps as a deterrence? Very hard to say. How can anyone calculate how many youths have not committed crimes because they are scared of boot camp?
   Hinweis: Z. 68–72

9. … worry that the camps might increase problematic feelings.
   Evidence: Or is it more likely that such a system … will develop frustration, a feeling of inferiority and, of course, aggression? These seem to be exactly the factors that lead young people to commit crime in the first place.
   Hinweis: Z. 80–86

10. false
    Evidence: Canadians have chosen something else
    Hinweis: Z. 90/91

11. … inform the reader about boot camps for young criminals.
    Hinweis: Im Text ist nirgends von Boot Camps in Europa die Rede, die dritte Möglichkeit scheidet daher aus. „Wilderness camps" werden zwar kurz erwähnt – es ist aber nicht das Hauptziel des Textes, sie mit Boot Camps zu vergleichen. Die zweite Möglichkeit ist daher die richtige – der Text will allgemein über Boot Camps für junge Kriminelle informieren.

Reading Test 10: Bog Child

1. false
   Evidence: He didn't loop the long way round, but headed straight to the sentry hut.
   Hinweis: Z. 2

2. false
   Evidence: He'd never once considered the possibility that somebody other than Owain might be on duty.
   Hinweis: Z. 9/10

3. … is only joking.
Evidence: "Hello, Mr Terrorist. […] How's the rebellion going?" / "I'm serious." / "Owain. Honest." / "You're pulling my leg, Fergus."
Hinweis: Z. 15–17; Z. 19; Z. 25
Hier kommen mehrere Textstellen infrage – es reicht aber, wenn du eine davon angibst. Die Anrede „Hello, Mr Terrorist" und die Frage „How's the rebellion going?" sind ironisch gemeint – Owain glaubt nicht wirklich, dass Fergus ein Terrorist ist.

4. … in a very critical condition.
Evidence: Conscious? Kind of. We expect to hear he's gone into a coma any day.
Hinweis: Z. 43

5. … he was hoping they might make Joey stop his hunger strike.
Evidence: But they said if I did this for them, they'd send in the word to Joey to order him off his strike.
Hinweis: Z. 54/55

6. … in order to protect Owain.
Evidence: You. They threatened you.
Hinweis: Z. 69

7. … he has a bad conscience.
Evidence: I can't stand the guilt. It's killing me.
Hinweis: Z. 79

8. … find out what is inside the packets.
Evidence: We'll open them.
Hinweis: Z. 82/83

▶ Lösungen zum Bereich Wortschatz – Verfügbarkeit sprachlicher Mittel

Aufgabe 1

Hinweis: Hier geht es darum, Wortfelder zu erarbeiten. In Teilaufgabe a) sollst du die vorgegebenen Wörter den entsprechenden Oberbegriffen zuordnen. Teilaufgabe b) ist eine Fortführung des ersten Teils der Aufgabe. Auch hier sollst du eine Mindmap zu einem Oberbegriff anlegen. Allerdings sind die Wörter hier nicht vorgegeben, sondern du musst dir selbst die entsprechenden Begriffe überlegen.

a)

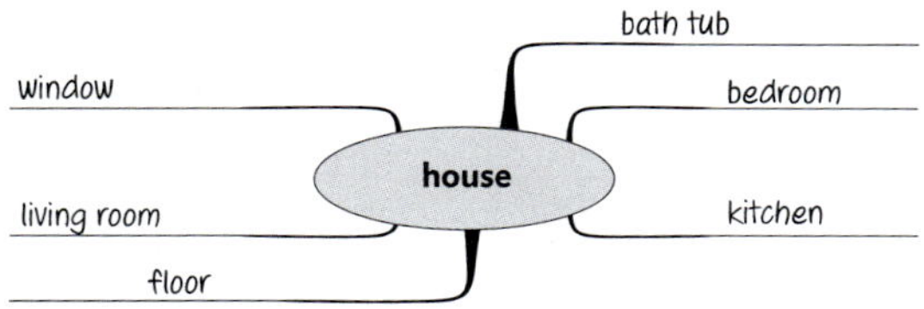

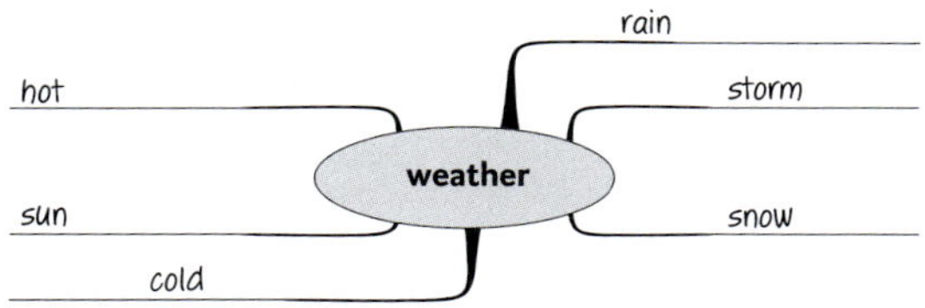

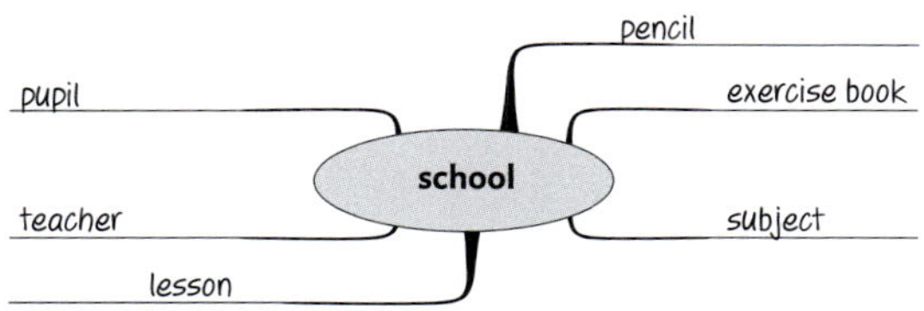

b) *Beispiellösung:*

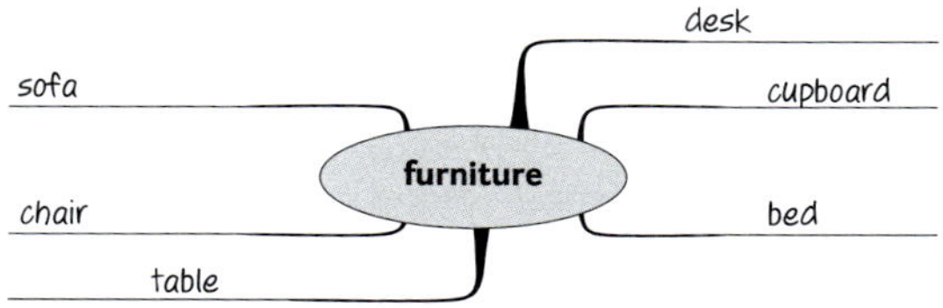

Aufgabe 2

Hinweis: In dieser Aufgabe sollst du eine Tabelle vervollständigen, in der es um Nationalitäten, Länder und Sprachen geht. Denke daran, dass man diese Wörter im Englischen immer großschreibt.

the people	the country	the language
(the) English	England	**English**
(the) French	**France**	**French**
(the) Spanish	**Spain**	**Spanish**
(the) Italians	**Italy**	Italian
(the) Americans	**United States of America / United States / USA / America**	**English**
(the) Germans	Germany	**German**
(the) Dutch	**the Netherlands**	Dutch
(the) Turkish	**Turkey**	Turkish
(the) Canadians	**Canada**	**French, English**

Aufgabe 3

Hinweis: Nachdem du die Tabelle in Aufgabe 2 ausgefüllt hast, wird dir die Lösung dieser Aufgabe nicht mehr schwerfallen. Wenn du dir bei den englischen Begriffen für Land, Leute und Sprache nicht sicher bist, dann schreibe die Wörter in deine Vokabelkartei und lerne sie.

Peter moved to Poland two months ago. As he doesn't speak any Polish yet, he started a language course last week. The other students in his course are from many different countries. Jenny, for example, is from Manchester in the North of **England**. She's **English**. Jan comes from Amsterdam in **the Netherlands**. He's **Dutch**. Ismael is **Turkish**. He's from Istanbul. Istanbul is in **Turkey**. Then there's Pietro. He comes from Rome, the capital of **Italy**. Pietro only speaks **Italian**. Louise used to live in Paris. She's **French**. Many people in **France** only speak **French**, but Louise speaks Portuguese and English, too. José is from Madrid, the capital of **Spain**. He isn't **Spanish**, because he was born in Mexico, where people also speak **Spanish**. The girl Peter likes the most is called Sophia. She's **Canadian**. She was born in Quebec. That is why her native language isn't English, but **French**.

Aufgabe 4

Hinweis: Hier kannst du das Wortfeld „Berufe" wiederholen. Deine Aufgabe ist es, den neun Berufen die passenden Elemente (z.B. Personen oder Gegenstände) zuzuordnen, mit denen die Personen in ihrem Beruf zu tun haben.

❶	❷	❸	❹	❺	❻	❼	❽	❾
H	I	E	F	G	C	B	D	A

Aufgabe 5

Hinweis: Hier musst du einen Lückentext über London vervollständigen. Lies dir zuerst den ganzen Text durch, damit du weißt, wovon er handelt. Erst im Anschluss füllst du die Lücken mit Wörtern, die in den Kontext passen. Als Hilfe ist der erste Buchstabe eines jeden Wortes vorgegeben. Wenn du alle Lücken gefüllt hast, liest du dir am besten den gesamten Text noch einmal durch, um zu überprüfen, ob er inhaltlich einen Sinn ergibt und auch grammatikalisch korrekt ist.

London is the **capital** of England. It's a very **large** city with **many** interesting **sights**. It's also a city with a great nightlife. There are lots of **cinemas**, theatres, and, of course, clubs, **restaurants** and pubs. There is **always** lots to do and see. You can **visit** Buckingham Palace or see Downing Street where the prime minister **lives**. There is also a big wheel called the "London Eye". From the **top** of it there is a **fantastic** view over London, but it is very **high**! The **best** way to see London, though, is on **foot** or by a city tour on a **red** double-decker **bus**. London is a **wonderful** city – everyone should visit it **sometime / someday**.

Aufgabe 6

Hinweis: Auch hier ist ein Lückentext auszufüllen. In der ersten Lücke sollst du das Datum ergänzen. Denk daran, dass man „the" und „of" zwar spricht – „On the 5th of August" – aber nicht schreibt. Bei Mengenangaben wie „many bottles" ist es wichtig, dass du die Präposition „of" ergänzt: "many bottles of water".

On **5(th) August / August 5(th)** last year I went to Paris for the day. The flight was only 75 minutes long. In Paris, I bought a lot of things. They had lovely biscuits, so I got six **packets of** very nice ones. Paris was very hot, so I had to carry a **bottle of** water around with me all the time. I drank so many **bottles of** water I didn't count them all. I bought my mum a **jar of** French marmalade and my dad a **litre of** French wine. I had a great time!

Aufgabe 7

Hinweis: Achte darauf, dass du die Wörter in der Form einträgst, wie sie in den jeweiligen Satz passen. Bei ❶ und ❽ brauchst du z. B. den Plural.

❶	*	*	*	I	N	H	A	B	I	T	A	N	T	S
❷	*	*	*	*	*	*	G	O	L	D	*	*	*	*
❸	*	*	*	*	*	*	*	B	U	F	F	A	L	O
❹	*	*	*	*	*	*	*	D	R	E	A	M	*	*
❺	*	L	I	B	E	R	T	Y	*	*	*	*	*	*
❻	*	*	*	*	*	*	S	L	A	V	E	R	Y	*
❼	*	*	*	*	E	Q	U	A	L	*	*	*	*	*
❽	I	M	M	I	G	R	A	N	T	S	*	*	*	*

The famous American singer who won the Nobel Prize for Literature in 2016 is **Bob Dylan**.

Aufgabe 8

Hinweis: Bei dieser Aufgabe musst du das Gegenteil des unterstrichenen Wortes finden. Achte darauf, dass der Satz mit dem „opposite" immer noch Sinn gibt.

a) The train is **early**.
b) I have just **missed** the last bus home.
c) I've **found** my watch.
d) He's **sold** a car.
e) Julie's water bottle is **empty**.

Aufgabe 9

Hinweis: Hier musst du ein Wort mit der gleichen oder einer ähnlichen Bedeutung finden. Achte darauf, dass dieses Wort auch in den Satzzusammenhang passt.

a) The **border** between the USA and Mexico is 1,954 miles long.
b) The **whole** world was shocked when the popular actor died so young.
c) Last year he **finally/eventually** got the academy award he had been hoping for for so long.
d) **Very tall / Very big / Enormous** skyscrapers shape the skyline of Manhattan.
e) Do you have any plans to spend some time **in another country/ in a foreign country** after your GCSEs?
f) If you live in an English-speaking country for a few months, your English will **get better** significantly.
g) Just a few more miles. We're **nearly** there!
h) When I saw her face, I knew **immediately** what had happened.

Aufgabe 10

Hinweis: Probiere verschiedene Möglichkeiten aus, ein Wort zu erklären. Du kannst in deiner Definition z. B. eine Umschreibung oder ein Synonym des Wortes verwenden, es mithilfe des Gegenteils erklären oder durch ein gutes Beispiel deutlich machen, was man darunter versteht. Bei dieser Aufgabe gibt es natürlich sehr viele verschiedene Lösungsmöglichkeiten, diese Musterlösung ist nur ein Beispiel.

a) It is a period of a hundred years.

b) “To shake hands” means to take somebody’s hand in order to say “hello” or as a kind of greeting.

c) This is a set of medical materials which you need in an emergency.

d) “Rubbish” is another word for “garbage”, “waste” or “litter”.

e) A school subject is a special lesson at school where you learn something in a certain field, e. g. Biology, Maths or P.E.

f) “To explore” means to have a close / proper look at something which you have not experienced before.

Aufgabe 11

Hinweis: Hier gibt es noch weitere Lösungsmöglichkeiten. Falls du in deiner Lösung ein Wort aufgeführt hast, das nicht in dieser Liste steht, dann prüfe anhand deines Wörterbuches, ob deine Lösung richtig ist.

verb	noun(s)	adjective(s)	verb + preposition
to know	**knowledge**	**known, knowing**	**to know about/of (sth/sb)**
to educate	**education, educator**	educational, educated	**to educate (sb) in/about/on (sth)**
to mean	**meaning**	**meaningful, meaningless**	**to mean (sth) to (sb)**
to succeed	success	**successful**	**to succeed in (sth)**
to differ	**difference**	**different**	**to differ from (sth/sb)**
to vary	**variety**	various, varied	**to vary from (sth/sb), to vary in (sth)**
to act	**action, act, activity, actor/actress**	**active**	**to act as (sb), to act on (sth), to act like (sb)**
to speak	**speech, speaker**	spoken	**to speak about (sth/sb), to speak to/with/for (sb), to speak out**
to invite	**invitation**	inviting	**to invite (sb) to/for (sth)**

Aufgabe 12

✎ *Hinweis: Ähnlich wie in der Tabelle in der vorhergehenden Aufgabe musst du hier Wörter aus derselben Wortfamilie finden. Sieh dir die Sätze sorgfältig an, um herauszufinden, welche Wortart in der Lücke fehlt. Suche bei den Lücken mit Fragezeichen nach einer passenden Präposition.*

I really like music. I have never played a **musical** instrument in my life but I have always found **songs** fascinating. For me they are **interesting** in two ways. First, I find that as time goes **by** they remind me of things that have happened in my **life**. I remember my first girlfriend, **for** example, by a song that was always on the radio at that time. Secondly, I'm fascinated with what the lyrics really **mean**. It was only **recently**, for example, that I discovered what Bob Marley was singing about in his song "Buffalo Soldier". Buffalo soldiers were **Africans** who fought for the Americans against the Native Americans. June is also a **creative** but maybe not very **famous** singer-songwriter. Although I **probably** won't remember many of her songs in the future, I can relate to the **expression** of **feelings** in her lyrics and enjoy her live **performances**. If you ever find the time, listen to a song carefully and try to find **out** what it is about and why it was written – you'll probably find it interesting, too.

Aufgabe 13

✎ *Hinweis: Bei dieser Aufgabe musst du aus drei Begriffen den jeweils richtigen aussuchen und unterstreichen – die falschen Möglichkeiten sind in der untenstehenden Lösung nicht mehr angegeben. Bei den Teilaufgaben a) und g) musst du besonders aufpassen, denn hier tauchen in der Angabe gleich drei sogenannte „false friends" auf: „Meinung" heißt auf Englisch nämlich nicht „meaning", sondern „opinion". Auch das „Handy" wird auf Englisch nicht „handy" genannt, sondern „mobile (phone)" (das englische Wort „handy" gibt es zwar auch, es ist aber ein Adjektiv und bedeutet so viel wie „praktisch"). Das englische Wort „telly" hat ebenfalls nichts mit dem deutschen „Telefon" zu tun, sondern ist der umgangssprachliche Ausdruck für „television" (also für den Fernseher).*

a) Tim gave his <u>opinion</u> about the film to his friends.

b) On the <u>back</u> of the letter there was a small picture.

c) I'm going to <u>go</u> to London by train.

d) We need to talk about the problems we have got.

e) It was terribly wet in Scotland when we went there.

f) Can I watch television, please?

g) Chloe isn't home yet but you can call her on her mobile.

h) I'm really looking forward to our holiday in Canada – I'm sure it'll be great!

i) Could you turn off the computer before you go to bed, please?

Hinweis: Die Aufgaben 14 bis 16 sind ähnlich aufgebaut wie im MSA, d. h., sie bestehen aus einer Mischung aus Multiple-Choice-Aufgaben und Lückensätzen. Mit diesen Übungen kannst du also testen, ob du schon „fit" für die Prüfung bist.

Aufgabe 14

a) … use / go on / surf / connect to / are on …

b) about

c) … answer …

d) keep

e) reliable

f) pay

g) … clever / intelligent / good / sensible /…

h) give

i) … employers / companies / firms /…

j) for

Aufgabe 15

a) … happens …

b) probably

c) hire

d) … rules …

e) of

f) … came / arrived / landed …

g) get
h) simply
i) payment
j) prefer
k) … opinion(s) / view(s) / take /…

Aufgabe 16

a) collecting
b) … piece / slip / sheet …
c) forget
d) in front of
e) perfectly
f) Believe / Trust …
g) … mood …
h) at
i) … slowly / clearly /…
j) follow

Lösungen zum Bereich Grammatik – Sprachliche Korrektheit

Allgemeiner Hinweis: Die Übungsaufgaben beziehen sich jeweils auf bestimmte grammatische Strukturen. Wenn du hier noch Schwierigkeiten haben solltest, lies am besten das entsprechende Kapitel in der Kurzgrammatik auf MyStark durch, bevor du die Aufgaben löst. Das relevante Kapitel ist jeweils in der Aufgabe und im „Hinweis" zur Lösung angegeben.

Aufgabe 1

Hinweis: Sieh dir die Situation auf dem Bild genau an und überlege, welche der Präpositionen zu den Sätzen a) bis f) passen. Falls du denkst, dass mehrere für eine Lücke infrage kommen, gehe zu den nächsten Sätzen und entscheide dich erst, wenn du die anderen Lücken gefüllt hast. Wenn du im Ausschlussverfahren vorgehst, gibt es überall nur eine mögliche Lösung. Erklärungen und Beispiele zu den Präpositionen findest du in der Kurzgrammatik unter 1.4.

a) The family is sitting **in front of** their tent, **beside** their car.

b) Everybody is **outside**, there is no one **inside** the tent.

c) There is a tree **behind** the car.

d) The little girl is sitting **between** her sister and brother.

e) There's lots of food **on** the table and a bowl of water **under** the table.

f) The father is looking **at** the dog.

Aufgabe 2

Hinweis: Hier musst du selbst überlegen, welche Präpositionen in die Lücken passen. Achtung, zahlreiche Verben stehen immer mit bestimmten Präpositionen (z. B. „to wait for", „to pick up"); diese solltest du auch gleich als Einheit lernen und am besten so in dein Vokabelheft oder Karteisystem eintragen.

a) I got a letter **from** my brother today. He put the wrong stamps **on** the letter. As no one was **at** home when the postman came, he left a note **on/at** the front door. I had to go **to** the post office and pick **up** the letter myself. I had to pay 50 p **for** the extra postage.

b) It happened **on** 31st October, **at** about nine o'clock **in** the evening. Amy had been waiting **for** her boyfriend **for** what seemed like hours. He had said he'd be there **by** six at the latest. She was just about to go **back** home, when he suddenly appeared right **next to/in front of/behind** her. Of course she was scared – but what else should you be **on** Halloween?

Aufgabe 3

Hinweis: Konjunktionen dienen dazu, das Verhältnis zwischen Sätzen bzw. Satzteilen deutlich zu machen. Überlege bei jeder Lücke, ob eine zeitliche Beziehung ausgedrückt werden soll (z. B. mit „after", „before" usw.) oder vielleicht ein Gegensatz (z. B. „but") oder eine Einschränkung (z. B. „although"). Die verschiedenen Bedeutungen und die Verwendung der Konjunktionen kannst du in Kapitel 1.5 der Grammatik nachschlagen.

a) **As soon as** James McAlister has finished school, he is **both** going to apply for an internship with the American company Open Access Music Library, **and** take a job with the Scottish firm UnlimitedAccess.co.uk. **Although** he is in Scotland, he will be able to work with the American company online, **but** he will have to fly to the States to present himself **before** he can start to work for them.

b) **As** Caroline's mother is a journalist, that is the last thing Caroline wants to become! **After** finishing school Caroline is going to study medicine in London, **and** then she hopes she will be able to get some practical experience working in America **or** Canada. **While** still at school she has been doing some voluntary work at a hospital near her home. **Before** she can study medicine, though, she really needs to study hard.

Aufgabe 4

Hinweis: Falls du Probleme bei der Verwendung der Modalverben hast, hilft dir Kapitel 1.6 der Kurzgrammatik weiter. In Teilaufgabe a) geht es um die Modalverben im „present tense", bei Aufgabe b) musst du auch die Ersatzformen der Modalverben kennen, die du z. B. für die Bildung der Vergangenheit oder Zukunft brauchst.

a) We **can** fly or go by train, but we **can't** go during your exams – that's clear – so we'll go on 26th July for a week. If you want to go to London, you **have to/must** return the form to me by Monday. You **needn't** bring any money until next week – I'm not collecting it before then. But don't forget, I **must/have to** have the forms on Monday.

b) **1** can't **2** May
3 will be able to **4** might
5 has to **6** can't
7 needn't **8** is allowed to
9 could **10** would
11 should **12** will be allowed to
13 mustn't **14** could
15 would

Aufgabe 5

Hinweis: Das „present progressive" wird hier verwendet, um zu beschreiben, was auf einem Bild gerade passiert. Wenn du dir bei der Bildung dieser Zeitform nicht mehr sicher bist, sieh in der Grammatik in Kapitel 2.1 unter „present progressive" nach.

a) The man in the van **is selling** ice creams.

b) The ice-cream man **is looking** out of the side window.

c) Another man **is standing** behind the ice-cream van.

d) The man behind the ice-cream van **is calling/is phoning** a friend.

e) No one **is buying** an ice cream.

f) The ice-cream man **is waiting** for customers.

Aufgabe 6

Hinweis: Beispiele zu den Signalwörtern für die Verwendung des „simple present" oder des „present progressive" findest du in der Grammatik unter 2.1.

a) Karen <u>always</u> **walks** to school.

b) She **is carrying** her large school bag <u>now</u>.

c) Karen and her family **are flying** to England <u>this year</u>. <u>Normally</u>, they **drive** there.

d) Karen's dad **is working** on his computer <u>at the moment</u>. When he is busy he <u>never</u> **talks/speaks** to anybody.

Aufgabe 7

Hinweis: In dieser Aufgabe werden die unregelmäßigen Vergangenheitsformen abgefragt. Bestimmt hast du in deinem Englischbuch eine Übersicht über die unregelmäßigen Verben; auch in den Kapiteln 2.1 und 3.4 der Kurzgrammatik findest du einige Beispiele. Du musst sie auswendig lernen. Vielleicht hilft es dir, die unregelmäßigen Verben in deine Vokabelkartei aufzunehmen.

		simple past	present perfect
a)	be	was/were	has/have been
b)	have	had	has/have had
c)	say	said	has/have said
d)	go	went	has/have gone
e)	take	took	has/have taken
f)	write	wrote	has/have written
g)	buy	bought	has/have bought

Aufgabe 8

Hinweis: Es ist wichtig, dass du diese Signalwörter gut kennst. Sie helfen dir, die zeitliche Situation richtig einzuordnen und die passende Zeitform auszuwählen. Du solltest sie am besten auswendig kennen, denn dies spart dir in Klassenarbeiten und in der Prüfung viel Zeit. Falls du hier Fehler gemacht hast, sieh dir die Signalwörter noch einmal gut an und wiederhole die Übung in einigen Wochen.

simple past	present perfect
five years ago in 2010 last month last week yesterday	already ever for three weeks how long just not … yet since May

Aufgabe 9

Hinweis: Das deutsche Wort „seit“ kannst du im Englischen mit „since“ oder „for“ übersetzen. Welches Wort passt, hängt davon ab, ob ein Zeitpunkt oder eine Zeitspanne beschrieben wird. Für einen Zeitpunkt verwendest du „since“, für einen Zeitraum „for“. Wenn dir die Unterscheidung schwerfällt, hilft dir das Lernvideo weiter.

since 2012

for six days

since last weekend

for three hours

since last summer

since my birthday

since Easter

for a long time

for many years

for seven days

Aufgabe 10

Hinweis: Bei dieser Aufgabe helfen dir die Signalwörter aus Aufgabe 8, die richtige Zeit auszuwählen. Bei den Teilaufgaben b) und e) solltest du die „progressive“-Form verwenden, da hier die Dauer der Handlung im Vordergrund steht (vgl. auch Kapitel 2.1 der Kurzgrammatik).

a) Yesterday, I **went** to the cinema.

b) She **has been writing** since 3 o'clock.

c) He **has** just **finished** his homework.

d) It was many years ago that I **visited** America.

e) How long **have** you **been waiting**?

f) In 1999 we **drove** to Italy. Then two years ago we **flew**. We **have** not **been** there since then.

g) Last week we **had** our last English lesson before our exams.

Aufgabe 11

Hinweis: Um zu entscheiden, ob du „simple past“ oder „past perfect“ verwenden musst, musst du immer überlegen, welche Handlung zuerst stattfand. Manchmal helfen dir Adverbien wie „after“ oder „before“ dabei, manchmal musst du das aber auch aus dem Zusammenhang erschließen. Wenn du zwei Handlungen vergleichst, die zu verschiedenen Zeiten in der Vergangenheit passierten, so steht die frühere („vorzeitige") Handlung im „past perfect" und die spätere im „simple past". Die Regeln zur Bildung und Verwendung dieser Zeitformen findest du auch in der Kurzgrammatik im Kapitel 2.1.

a) After Ellis Island **had served** as a fort and execution site it **became** an immigration center in 1892.

b) It was there that doctors and officials **decided** the futures of all those who **had left** Europe in the hope of a new life in America.

c) After they **had passed** through the baggage room, the newcomers **climbed** the long stairs up to the Great Hall.

d) Once the doctors **had examined** everybody, officials **came** and **questioned** them.

e) When they **had given** the right answers, they **started** to explore the New World.

Aufgabe 12

Hinweis: In den Aufgaben 5 bis 11 hast du die verschiedenen Zeitformen der Gegenwart und Vergangenheit geübt. In dieser gemischten Aufgabe kannst du nun überprüfen, wie sicher du die verschiedenen Formen anwenden kannst. Als Hilfestellung sind in der Musterlösung die Signalwörter unterstrichen. Mache aber auch nicht den Fehler, dich blind auf die Signalwörter zu verlassen und „automatisch" bestimmte Formen einzusetzen. Denke dich immer in die Situation des Textes hinein und versuche die zeitlichen Zusammenhänge nachzuvollziehen. Beachte, dass in einem Blog immer der aktuellste Eintrag oben steht.
Falls du noch Fragen hast, wann man welche Form verwendet, hilft dir das Kapitel 2.1 der Kurzgrammatik weiter. Bei vielen Lücken geht es um den Unterschied zwischen „simple past" und „present perfect". Zu diesem Thema gibt es übrigens auch ein Lernvideo.

July 3rd

We**'d been travelling/were travelling/(had) travelled** all day and arrived in Dover just in time for the ferry. We**'d been planning/'d planned** to sleep on the ferry but it **wasn't** really possible. We **got off** at Calais at about 3 o'clock this morning. Now we have to **wait** here in the ferry terminal for a few hours. Our bus **doesn't leave** until 6 o'clock.

June 17th

Someone **told** me a few days ago to buy a rail card. I **looked** on the internet last night and I **discovered** it **costs** £ 250 but it **means** we can **travel** by train anywhere in Europe for a month – and **sleep** on the trains overnight, too.

June 15th

Tina and I **have been buying/have bought** lots of things for our trip; I hope we can carry everything. Tina **doesn't have** a lot of money so we're going to camp. We **borrowed** a tent and two rucksacks last weekend from my parents. But I **don't know** which clothes to take with me.

June 1st

I've been living/'ve lived in my student flat since September. I**'ve met** a lot of people and I now **have** many new friends. I **asked** Tina yesterday if she wanted to come with me to the Continent in the summer holidays. She **said** she'd love to come.

Aufgabe 13

Hinweis: Bei zukünftigen Handlungen musst du überlegen, ob sie geplant sind („going to-future"), oder ob es sich um einen spontanen Entschluss, eine Vorhersage oder ein Ereignis handelt, das in der Zukunft eintreten wird, ohne dass man das beeinflussen kann („will-future"). Eine ausführlichere Erklärung zu den Zeitformen der Zukunft findest du am Ende von Kapitel 2.1 der Grammatik oder im Lernvideo. Dass man manchmal auch „simple present" oder „present progressive" für zukünftige Handlungen verwenden kann, brauchst du in dieser Aufgabe nicht zu berücksichtigen.

a) I'll send Karen an e-mail.
   Hinweis: Wie auf dem Notizzettel angegeben, ist die E-Mail eine spontane Idee. Daher verwendet man das „will-future".

b) I am going to go to Venice on 27th December.
   Hinweis: Eine geplante Reise ist ein typisches Beispiel für die Verwendung des „going to-future".

c) I am going to go to the cinema with friends.
   Hinweis: Auch die Verabredung mit Freunden fürs Kino ist ein Plan für die Zukunft. Daher musst du das „going to-future" verwenden.

d) I am going to go to the dentist tomorrow at 4.30 p.m.
Hinweis: Der Zahnarztbesuch ist ebenfalls ein Plan. Da hier schon ein Termin vereinbart wurde, ist das „going to-future" die richtige Zeitform.

e) Next week the school holidays will start.
Hinweis: Der Ferienbeginn ist ein Ereignis in der Zukunft, auf das man keinen Einfluss hat. Hier wird das „will-future" verwendet.

f) Grandma will be 70 next month.
Hinweis: Altersangaben in der Zukunft sind ebenfalls typische Beispiele für Ereignisse, die man nicht beeinflussen kann. Somit ist auch in diesem Fall das „will-future" die richtige Wahl.

g) I am going to meet Luke at 11 o'clock.
Hinweis: Eine Verabredung ist ein geplantes Ereignis in der Zukunft. Hier ist es erforderlich, das „going to-future" zu verwenden.

h) I'll buy Julie a present sometime next week.
Hinweis: Dieses Vorhaben ist kein richtiger Plan. Du erkennst dies an der ungenauen Zeitangabe „sometime next week". In einem solchen Fall steht das „will-future".

Aufgabe 14

Hinweis: Bei dieser Aufgabe geht es ebenfalls um verschiedene Zeitformen, die allerdings im Passiv stehen. Falls du die Regeln zu den Passivformen noch einmal wiederholen möchtest, sieh dir das Lernvideo an und/oder lies dir Kapitel 2.2 in der Grammatik durch.

1 will be decorated
Hinweis: „Next week" weist auf eine Handlung in der Zukunft hin.
→ „will-future"

2 have to be done
Hinweis: „Before then" bezieht sich auf „next week", d. h., etwas muss (= „to have to") noch bis nächste Woche getan werden.

3 has been given
Hinweis: „Already" zeigt, dass die Handlung schon in der Vergangenheit begonnen hat und noch andauert. → „present perfect"

4 has been moved
Hinweis: Die Handlung bezieht sich auch auf „already" (vgl. vorhergehenden Satz), d. h., sie hat in der Vergangenheit begonnen und man kann evtl. ein Ergebnis sehen: Die Möbel stehen nicht mehr in der Wohnung bzw. sind zur Seite geräumt worden. → „present perfect"

5 will be taken off
Hinweis: „Later" weist darauf hin, dass die Handlung erst noch stattfinden wird. → „will-future"

6 was last painted
Hinweis: „Many years ago" ist ein Signalwort für eine abgeschlossene Handlung. → „simple past"

7 was given
Hinweis: „Last year" verweist auf eine vergangene Handlung, die abgeschlossen ist. → „simple past"

8 will be covered up
Hinweis: „Soon" ist ein Hinweis darauf, dass die Handlung erst noch stattfinden wird. → „will-future"

9 has been done
Hinweis: „Once" ist hier eine Konjunktion mit der Bedeutung „sobald". Es zeigt hier an, dass eine Handlung gerade vorbei sein wird. → „present perfect"

10 has been completed
Hinweis: Auch mit „until" (= „bis") wird eine Handlung beschrieben, die in der Zukunft gerade vorbei sein wird. → „present perfect"

Aufgabe 15

Hinweis: Bei diesen Sätzen musst du aufpassen, dass du das Verb in die richtige Zeit setzt. Beachte die Signalwörter, die dir Hinweise auf die Zeit geben.

a) English **is spoken** all over the world.
Hinweis: Die Aussage bezieht sich auf die Gegenwart.

b) Last week a new crew **was sent** up to the ISS.
Hinweis: „Last week" ist ein Signalwort für „simple past".

c) Up to now Atlantis **has not been discovered.**
Hinweis: „Up to now" weist auf eine Handlung hin, die noch nicht abgeschlossen ist. → „present perfect"

d) The door should always **be locked.**
Hinweis: Die Lücke folgt hier auf das Modalverb „should", d. h., du musst einen Infinitiv im Passiv bilden.

Aufgabe 16

Hinweis: In der Kurzgrammatik (Kapitel 3.1 bis 3.3) findest du viele Beispiele für Ausdrücke, auf die entweder der Infinitiv oder die -ing-*Form folgt. Allerdings enthält die Grammatik natürlich nicht alle englischen Verben; du solltest daher immer gleich in deinem Vokabellernsystem notieren, ob ein Verb mit Infinitiv oder mit der* -ing-*Form (oder mit beidem) verwendet wird.*

❶ **Climbing** is a good sport, but you have **to be** fit. If you want to learn **to climb**, it's probably best to start **doing/to do** it on a climbing wall. There is no chance **of falling** very far because you'll have a rope **to stop/stopping** you from **doing** that. After **learning to climb** on our wall we'll take you to a real mountain. We look forward **to seeing** you on our course.

❷ **Windsurfing** is fun. On our courses we'll show you how to windsurf from the very beginning – you just shouldn't be afraid **of getting/to get** wet. Before **going** onto the lake you'll learn how **to control** the windsurfer on the land. In this way, you'll avoid **spending** many hours in the lake trying to pull yourself back onto the windsurfer.

❸ Have you ever been on a horse? **Horse(back) riding/Horse-riding/Riding a horse** is a very nice way **to see/of seeing** the countryside. Our horses are friendly and there's very little danger **of having** an accident with one. You'll never forget **getting** onto a horse for the first time.

Aufgabe 17

Hinweis: Bei dieser Aufgabe musst du überlegen, welche Fragen wohl gestellt wurden, um die angegebenen Antworten zu erhalten. Falls du nachlesen willst, wie Fragesätze gebildet werden, sieh in Kapitel 2.1 der Grammatik (unter „Bildung von Fragen im ‚simple present' bzw. im ‚present progressive'") nach. Bei der Wahl der passenden Zeitformen und Verben kannst du dich an der Antwort orientieren und einfach Zeitform und Verb übernehmen.

a) What is the advert for?

b) How many bands are playing?
Hinweis: Die Fragen "Who is playing?" oder "Which bands are playing?" passen nicht, denn dann würde man auch die Namen der Bands in der Antwort erwarten.

c) Where is the party (night)?
or: Where does the party (night) take place?

d) When does the party (night) start?
or: What time does the party (night) begin?

e) How much does the party (night) cost?
or: How much does it cost?
or: How much is a ticket for the party?

f) Why do we/you/people have to leave just/shortly before 3 o'clock?
or: Why does the party (have to) end at 3 a.m.?

Aufgabe 18

Hinweis: Bei dieser Aufgabe musst du die vorgegebenen Sätze verneinen. Du kannst dabei sowohl Kurz- als auch Langformen verwenden. (Zur Bildung der Verneinung in den verschiedenen Zeitformen siehe auch Kapitel 2.1 der Kurzgrammatik.)

a) They are not/aren't learning English.

b) Mary does not/doesn't drive a fast car.

c) We cannot/can't take the next train to Manchester.

d) My homework is not/isn't very hard today.

e) Noah does not/doesn't play football every weekend.

f) I am not/I'm not going to go to the theatre.

g) We have not got/haven't got your telephone number.

h) Jenny will not/won't make the cakes.

i) I did not/didn't read my new book for hours last night.

j) Lucy did not/didn't arrive late for her doctor's appointment.

Aufgabe 19

Hinweis: Bei dieser Aufgabe musst du entscheiden, um welchen Typ von if-Satz es sich jeweils handelt. Welche Typen es gibt und welche Verbformen in Hauptsatz und if-Satz stehen, kannst du in Kapitel 4.2 der Grammatik nachschlagen. Zur Wiederholung dieses Grammatikthemas kannst du dir auch das Lernvideo ansehen.

Hi Amelia,
If I had more time, I **would write/could write/'d write** a much longer e-mail to you. But I haven't, so this will be a short message. If you want a longer one, you **will have/'ll have** to wait until next week!
I was in London last week, as you know. If you **had been/'d been** there, we could have gone to the theatre together. But that's why I'm writing. If you have time, **do you want** to come to the theatre with me next weekend? I noticed two or three more shows that I would love to see. Would you be interested in going if I **got** tickets? If you **are**, phone me tomorrow evening – I can book them online.
Oh, I almost forgot. Maxime **would have come/could have come** with me last week if he hadn't had to fly to Paris to meet his mum ... but he wants to come with us next time if you **don't mind**.
I **will send/'ll send/can send** you the theatre details if you would like to see what's on.

Love, Sam

Aufgabe 20

Hinweis: Denke daran, dass es für die Verbformen in der indirekten Rede entscheidend ist, ob das einleitende Verb (hier z. B. „says“, „told us“) in der Gegenwart oder in der Vergangenheit steht. Auch bei Adverbien der Zeit (z. B. „today“) und des Ortes (z. B. „here“) musst du besonders aufpassen. Wenn du die Regeln nicht mehr ganz im Kopf hast, kannst du dir das Lernvideo ansehen und/oder in Kapitel 4.4 der Kurzgrammatik nachlesen.

a) He says that he wants to listen to the radio because his favourite group are in concert today.
Hinweis: Einleitungsverb im „simple present“: Die Verben in der indirekten Rede bleiben im „simple present“ und auch die Zeitangabe „today“ bleibt unverändert. Denke daran, die Pronomen anzupassen (z. B. „I“ → „he“).

b) She told us (that) she thought the book had been better than the film.
Hinweis: Einleitungsverb im „simple past": Das Verb muss in der indirekten Rede eine Zeitstufe zurückgesetzt werden (z. B. „simple present" → „simple past").

c) He said (that) they had lost the football match the day before. They had played badly.
Hinweis: Einleitungsverb im „simple past": Die Verbformen, Pronomen und die Zeitangabe „yesterday" müssen angepasst werden.

d) The man explained (that) he had been there when the accident had happened. It had been no one's fault.
Hinweis: Einleitungsverb im „simple past": Die Verben und die Ortsangabe „here" werden verändert.

Aufgabe 21

Hinweis: In dieser Aufgabe geht es noch einmal um die indirekte Rede. Bei beiden Texten steht das einleitende Verb in der Vergangenheit. Denke also daran, alle Verben eine Zeitstufe zurückzusetzen. Vergiss auch nicht, die Pronomen, Orts- und Zeitangaben – wo nötig – anzupassen.

a) George said that **that was** the only trophy **he had** ever won. **He didn't** need another reason to keep it, **did he**? It **sat** on a shelf and sometimes **he showed** people **his** greatest sporting award.

b) Katy asked why **she kept** the teddy bear. She answered (that) **she didn't** really know. **She had bought** it during **their** holiday **the year before** because it **looked** so happy. (She added that) it **sat there** above **her** sofa, **smiled** across the room and **made her** think of the nice holiday **they had had** in Sweden. There **was** no other reason for keeping it. It **was** just a souvenir.

▶ Lösungen zum Schreiben

Allgemeiner Hinweis: Für den Bereich „Schreiben“ ist es wichtig, dass du die Arbeitsschritte zum Verfassen eines Textes in Kapitel 5.1 des Trainingsbandes genau durchliest und dementsprechend arbeitest. Wenn du nach diesen Schritten vorgehst, wird es dir nicht mehr schwerfallen, einen guten Text zu schreiben. Beachte, dass es sich bei den Antworten zu den offenen Schreibaufgaben um Lösungsvorschläge handelt, die teilweise länger sind als z. B. in der Prüfung erforderlich. Deine Antworten werden in diesem Bereich also sicher von den vorgegebenen Texten abweichen. Die Beispiellösungen können dir aber wertvolle Ideen liefern und dienen dir zur Kontrolle.

Allgemeine Übungsaufgaben zum Bereich „Schreiben“

Aufgabe 1

Hinweis: Diese Aufgabe ist eine Vorbereitung auf das Schreiben eigener Texte. Alle Sätze sind zwar schon vollständig, durch weitere Adjektive, Adverbien bzw. Substantive kannst du sie aber noch lebendiger und interessanter machen. Mit dieser Technik kannst du auch deine eigenen Texte verbessern.

a) The **old** house was at the end of the **narrow** street.
b) Jane likes listening to **loud** music in her **small** bedroom.
c) The **young** boy ran away **quickly**.
d) We had a **terrible** meal in the **seafood** restaurant.
e) I didn't like the **horror** film because it was **so** boring.
f) My **summer** holiday was great.
g) There was a **long**, **sandy** beach with no one on it.
h) The sky was very **dark** before the storm.

Aufgabe 2

Hinweis: Sieh dir das Bild zuerst ganz in Ruhe an und mache dir Notizen. Wenn es dir schwerfällt, deine Ideen auf Englisch zu formulieren, kannst du auch zuerst Ideen auf Deutsch sammeln und diese dann ins Englische übertragen.

- **boy** – teenager, glasses, blond, notepad, exercise books, sad
- **people in the background** – 1 boy, 3 girls, laughing, one girl pointing, jeans, sunglasses, shorts, T-shirts

Aufgabe 3

Hinweis: Die Aufgaben helfen dir, auch auf Einzelheiten in dem Bild zu achten. Du kannst im ersten Schritt ganz einfache kurze Sätze schreiben. Um die Verbesserung dieses ersten Entwurfs geht es in der nächsten Aufgabe.

b) ▶ In the foreground there is a teenage boy.
▶ In the background I can see a group of teenagers.

c) ▶ The boy looks sad.
▶ He is carrying/holding papers and exercise books.
▶ He has his back to the other teenagers.
or: He stands with his back to the others.
or: He is standing away from the others with his back to them.

d) ▶ The other teenagers are wearing jeans and T-shirts. One girl is wearing shorts.
▶ They are standing near the building.
or: They are looking at the boy.
or: They are laughing and one girl is pointing at the boy.

Aufgabe 4

Hinweis: Jetzt geht es darum, deine Antworten aus der vorhergehenden Aufgabe weiter zu verbessern. Überlege bei jedem Satz, welche Informationen du noch geben könntest. Fällt dir noch ein Adjektiv ein, das beschreibt, wie der Junge oder die Teenager aussehen? Oder kannst du mit einem Adverb ausdrücken, wie sie etwas machen? Manchmal eignen sich auch eine Ortsangabe, weitere Substantive oder ein Relativsatz dazu, die Sätze interessanter zu machen.

b) ▶ In the foreground there is a **blond** teenage boy, **who is wearing a dark grey T-shirt**.
▶ In the background I can see a group of **four** teenagers **standing next to each other/close together**.

c) ▶ The boy looks very sad **and angry at the same time**.
▶ He is **firmly** holding papers and a **black** exercise book **in his arms**.

- ▶ He has his back to the other teenagers **and he is looking in the other direction**.

d) ▶ The other teenagers are wearing **casual** jeans and T-shirts, **which look like summer clothes**. One girl is wearing **denim** shorts.

- ▶ They are standing near the **school** building and they are looking **sneeringly** at the boy.
  or: … and they are looking at the boy **with something mean / nasty on their mind**.

Aufgabe 5

Hinweis: Sich selbst Fragen zu einem Bild zu stellen ist eine gute Möglichkeit, Ideen für eine Fantasiegeschichte zu sammeln. Stelle dir vor, du bist ein Reporter, der über die Personen auf dem Bild schreiben möchte. Welche Fragen müsste er stellen? Hier gibt es natürlich sehr viele verschiedene Möglichkeiten.

Possible questions:

- ▶ Why is the boy so sad / angry?
- ▶ What is the relationship between him and the other teenagers?
- ▶ Are they fighting about something that happened at school?
- ▶ Is / Was the boy in love with one of the people in the background?
- ▶ Is the boy a victim of bullying?
- ▶ What else is the boy wearing? Are they laughing at his trousers / shoes?
- ▶ What are the books and papers in the boy's hands about? Have they got something to do with the problem?

Aufgabe 6

Hinweis: Überlege dir nun jeweils eine Antwort auf die Fragen, die du in Aufgabe 5 gestellt hast. Hier sind deiner Fantasie keine Grenzen gesetzt. Die einzige Bedingung ist, dass du eine logische Erklärung für die Situation auf dem Bild geben musst. Es herrscht offensichtlich ein Konflikt zwischen dem Jungen und den restlichen Jugendlichen. Was passiert sein könnte, liegt ganz bei dir.

It's breaktime and Joe, the boy in the picture, has just run out of the big, white school building, firmly holding on to his black exercise book. It's one of the most precious things he owns, because it contains all the long letters he has ever written to Kaylee – and never given to her. How can he? Most of the time the other students make fun of him. He doesn't even know why the bullying started. All he knows is that it will get even worse, now that the whole school Facebook group has read his love letters to Kaylee. He doesn't dare turn around and look at her. The sneering look on her friends' faces would simply be too much.

Aufgabe 7

Hinweis: Nutze die Möglichkeit, in einer Mindmap zuerst einmal Ideen zu sammeln. Du musst nicht unbedingt die Vorgaben aus der Mindmap in der Aufgabenstellung nutzen. Wenn dir dazu nichts einfällt, kannst du dir auch andere Fragen überlegen.

a)

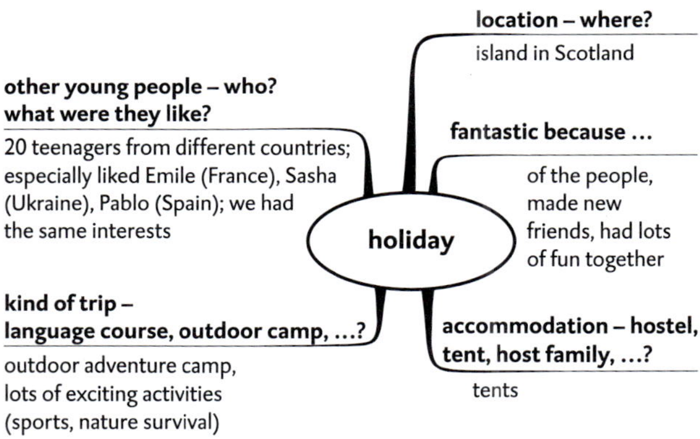

b) *Hinweis: Bevor du mit dem Formulieren der Nachricht beginnst, wähle sorgfältig aus, worüber du schreiben möchtest, und bringe deine Gedanken in eine gute Reihenfolge. Eine mögliche Gliederung wäre:*
- *Einleitung: Erkläre, warum du deinem Freund heute schreibst, und gib evtl. eine Entschuldigung, weil du lange nicht geschrieben hast.*
- *Hauptteil: Erzähle, was du in den Ferien erlebt hast.*
- *Schluss: Stelle Fragen an deinen Freund.*

Vergiss nicht, dass du deinen Freund/deine Freundin in die Nachricht einbeziehen solltest. Das kannst du mit Fragen ("What was your summer like?/ How was your summer?", "Have you been on holiday this year?") erreichen oder durch Äußerungen wie "I'm sure you would have liked that too" tun.

Hi Cameron,

Sorry that I've been so silent recently. I forgot to tell you that I went to an outdoor adventure camp during the holidays. It was my dad's idea to get me away from all my electronic gadgets ... I've just come back and I have to admit that it was a fantastic idea. I had such a great time. We – 20 kids from different European countries – spent two weeks on an island in Scotland. We were outside 24/7 doing all kinds of activities – lots of sports, but also unusual things like outdoor survival training. I'm sure my experience from all those online games helped me a lot there ☺. We had lots of fun and I made some cool new friends, like Pablo from Spain. Do you mind if I invite him to our group?

Best wishes,
Julian

140 words

Aufgabe 8

Hinweis: Diese Aufgabe ist wieder in zwei Schritte unterteilt, um dir zu helfen, eine solche kreative Schreibaufgabe leichter zu bewältigen. Nimm dir wirklich Zeit dafür, Ideen für die Geschichte zu sammeln. Überlege zuerst, was denn an diesem Tag Verrücktes passiert sein könnte. Wenn du einen ungefähren Plan hast, fällt dir bestimmt auch ein, wie eine passende Nachricht auf dem Telefon dazu lauten könnte.
Bevor du zu schreiben beginnst, überlege, ob du deine Geschichte aus der Ich-Perspektive oder in der dritten Person schreiben möchtest. Beginne dann entsprechend mit „message on my“ bzw. „his“ oder „her phone“. Beachte auch die Zeit, denn schon der Beginn „This day <u>was</u> just crazy. It all <u>started</u> ...“ signalisiert dir, dass die Geschichte in der Vergangenheit spielt. Die Verben stehen daher vermutlich meist im „past tense“. Wähle sorgfältig aus, welche Ideen du schließlich umsetzt, und schreibe nicht weniger als 120 Wörter.

a) ▶ **crazy:** went to a local talent show, had to think of a song spontaneously, promise: winner will perform the song in the stadium just before the next football match of the local team
▶ **message** from the chat group of the local sports club: "Come to the sports stadium at once. Don't ask why! I know you'll love it."

- what **happened** next: there were at least 100 boys and girls there, had to do some crazy things on stage in teams, only one member of each team got to the next round
- **end:** I was among the last five people, then they asked what date it was – April 1st, it was all just a joke
- **who:** a boy called Tom

b) *That day was just crazy. It all started with a message on his phone:* "Come to the sports stadium at once. Don't ask why! You'll love it." It appeared on Saturday morning in the chat group of his sports club. "Why not?", Tom thought and was at the stadium 20 minutes later. When he arrived, about 100 people were already waiting. The club leaders said that this was a singing and dancing competition to find the best talents for a performance that should take place right before the opening match of the football season. Tom was fascinated by the idea of singing in front of such a big audience. So he took part in all the crazy things they were told to do. He was delighted to be in the last round – until the final task: "What date is it today?" – It was April 1st. It was all just a joke. *137 words*

Aufgabe 9

Hinweis: Gehe am besten wieder so vor wie bei Aufgabe 8 und sammle zuerst Ideen, bevor du mit dem Schreiben beginnst. Was könnte ein Außerirdischer über das Leben auf der Erde denken? Welche Probleme könnte er/sie bekommen? Nachdem im ersten Satz der Außerirdische in der ersten Person spricht („I … my …"), musst du auch den Rest der Geschichte aus dieser Perspektive schreiben. Du kannst selbst entscheiden, ob X23 erzählt, was ihm/ihr an diesem Tag passiert ist (also in der Vergangenheit), oder ob die Geschichte in der Gegenwart erzählt wird.

Hi, I'm X23 and it's my first day on planet Earth. I'm sitting in this kind of stone box together with my new friend Dylan. He calls it "my room" – whatever that means. I rolled around town all day exploring this place. There are so many weird things, such as people sitting around and putting things into holes in their faces – in public!! Crazy. Dylan explained that this is what people on Earth call "eating". I am so hungry, too! I really need some electricity soon. But I couldn't find a socket for my plug anywhere – you know, the usual one with eight holes. I'm so glad I met Dylan in this electronics shop. He took me to his "room" with all these cool gadgets. He says he can fix my problem in no time. I hope he's right – beep, beep, beeeeeeeeeeeeep. *131 words*

Aufgabe 10

Hinweis: Anders als in den Aufgaben 8 und 9 ist hier nicht der erste Satz einer Geschichte bzw. eines Tagebucheintrags vorgegeben, sondern der letzte. Überlege zunächst, welche Informationen in diesem letzten Satz enthalten sind. Was könnten bei dieser Aufgabe z. B. die „red lights" sein? Vielleicht die Rücklichter eines Autos oder eines anderen Fahrzeuges? Oder das Leuchten in den Turnschuhen einer Person? Du kannst deiner Fantasie hier freien Lauf lassen, wichtig ist nur, dass die Lichter einen Bezug zu einer Person haben, um die es in deinem Tagebucheintrag geht. Einen Tagebucheintrag beginnst du normalerweise mit „Dear Diary,". Du kannst ihn auch mit einem Datum versehen.

Sunday, 24 June 20...

Dear Diary,

I'm still shaking while I'm writing these lines. I've just had the most frightening experience ever. I spent the evening with friends at the lake. First we had such a fantastic time – we were swimming and having fun in the water, and then had a barbecue by the lakeside. Just before leaving, Mike had this stupid idea to go for a last swim in the dark. We swam to the island in the middle of the lake. But what was that? Suddenly we saw a man searching all our belongings. I swam back as fast as I could but I had no chance. When I got out of the water and onto the street, I could only make out the rear lights of his car. *And those red lights were the last I ever saw of him.* *131 words*

Aufgabe 11

Hinweis: Bei dieser Aufgabe sollst du dich zu „Statements" äußern, in denen jemand eine eher provozierende Meinung vertritt. Überlege im ersten Schritt, welche Argumente dir für und gegen diese Aussagen einfallen. Du kannst dich entweder gleich für eine Haltung entscheiden und der Aussage zustimmen bzw. widersprechen oder erst einmal für beide Seiten Argumente sammeln.

❶ **Arguments for** 👍

- more boys and men watch action films than girls or women
- many girls find them boring

- girls prefer romantic films
- example: my family/ friends

Arguments against 👎
- just a stereotype
- girls can also be seen in the cinema when there's an action film on

❷ **Arguments for** 👍
- air traffic adds to global warming
- people need to be aware of this
- higher prices make them look for alternatives

Arguments against 👎
- air traffic is not the only cause of climate change
- some people have no alternative
- high prices are unfair

❸ **Arguments for** 👍

eating meat means that animals have to die
→ people who eat meat are responsible

Arguments against 👎
- meat-eaters do not actually kill the animals
- eating meat is normal behaviour for human beings
- animals also kill other animals → natural

❹ **Arguments for** 👍
- nothing for teenagers to do
- lonely: no friends in the same village
- no public transport
- dependent on parents/adults to get to the city
- no interesting events/clubs
- close community means supervision at all times

Arguments against 👎
- close to nature
- better for your health (clean air, less noise)
- safer for small children
- close community
- neighbours know and help each other

❺ **Arguments for** 👍
- ▶ they learn things they are interested in
- ▶ don't learn things they won't need
- ▶ highly motivated
- ▶ better marks

Arguments against 👎
- ▶ pupils don't know what they might need
- ▶ a general education is important
- ▶ you have to learn to deal with things you do not like

Aufgabe 12

Hinweis: Bei dieser Aufgabenstellung ist es nicht entscheidend, ob du der vorgegebenen Aussage zustimmst oder sie ablehnst. Dein Lehrer oder deine Lehrerin bewertet nicht deine Meinung, sondern nur, ob deine Argumente schlüssig sind und du sie gut auf Englisch ausdrücken kannst. Es ist auch gar nicht so wichtig, ob deine Antwort auch wirklich deine persönliche Meinung wiedergibt. Sieh dir deine Ideen für Argumente aus Aufgabe 11 an und entscheide dich für die beiden „Statements", zu denen du viel sagen kannst bzw. bei denen dir die meisten passenden Ausdrücke einfallen. Übrigens musst du den Aussagen auch nicht unbedingt völlig zustimmen bzw. sie komplett ablehnen, du kannst auch abwägen, z. B. mit „That depends …". Die Bezeichnungen ❶ bis ❺ beziehen sich auf die Reihenfolge der Aussagen in Aufgabe 11.

❶ **Zustimmung:** I agree, because there are far more boys than girls who like watching action films. You only have to look at my family. Whenever it is my brother's or father's turn to choose a film for the family film night, you can be sure it will be an action film. During the film they are fascinated by the speed of the action and the – mostly male – heroes, while my mother and I often fall asleep. *75 words*

Ablehnung: That is absolutely not true. It is only a stereotype that boys like action films and girls prefer romantic comedies. You only have to look at any cinema in the country when the next top-rated action film is shown. You will definitely see boys as well as girls. However, it might be true that girls and boys enjoy different things in an action film. *64 words*

❷ **Zustimmung:** It is true that air traffic is one of the causes of climate change. Therefore, it would be a good idea for passengers to have to pay twice as much for their flights. This would make them more aware of the damage they are causing to the environment and they might look for alternative means of travelling – especially if they are only travelling short distances and could also go by train. *71 words*

Ablehnung: I do not agree with this statement. Although I know that air traffic causes a certain amount of damage to the environment and is one of the causes of global warming, I think it would be wrong to increase the price of plane tickets that much. Some people have to go by plane, for example for their work or because their families live far away. It would be unfair to double the prices. *73 words*

❸ **Zustimmung:** Although the statement might be very extreme, I think it is true that people who eat meat are responsible for the death of another being – they are killers. Most people do not even think about the animals they are eating when biting into a steak or a burger. Furthermore, the killing of the animals is not the only negative aspect. Consumers who like to buy cheap meat make sure that the lives of animals are often torture, too.

78 words

Abwägende/ablehnende Haltung: On the one hand it is right, of course, that animals have to die if people eat meat, even though the person eating the beef steak is not actually involved in the process of killing the cow. On the other hand, however, it makes a difference to me what kind of meat someone eats. I would not call someone a killer who only buys meat if he/she is sure the animals had a good life and were treated with care. *80 words*

❹ **Zustimmung:** I am of the same opinion as I have lived in a small village all my life. There is nothing for teenagers to do, especially if no other young people of the same age live in this village. Whenever they want to go out and meet friends, their parents have to drive them, because the only public transport available is the school bus in the morning and afternoon.

68 words

Abwägende/ablehnende Haltung: As I see it, it depends on someone's age. For small children it is a great pleasure to grow up in a small village, because they can play outside and get to know nature. For older people it might also be very nice to live in a close community in which people know each other and are ready to help their neighbours. However, living in a small village is probably difficult for teenagers who want some action in their lives. *79 words*

❺ **Zustimmung:** That is a great idea. This way pupils would not have to study so much for subjects which they do not like and think they will never need in the future. I also think that there would not be any bad marks because pupils would study more for subjects which are interesting to them. *54 words*

Ablehnung: That sounds great but I think it would be bad for the pupils, because they would only choose the subjects they like and subjects they are good at. However, I think pupils need to study all subjects because when they are young they cannot know what might be important and necessary for their future jobs, for example. *56 words*

Aufgabe 13

Hinweis: Falls du Probleme hast, dich für eine Möglichkeit zu entscheiden, sieh dir die Wendungen zu Briefen und E-Mails in Kapitel 5.3 an. Überlege immer zuerst, ob du an diese Person einen persönlichen Brief schreiben würdest, weil du sie gut kennst, oder ob es sich um einen offiziellen Anlass handelt.

a) Hi Carlos,
Hinweis: Du kennst Carlos gut und schreibst ihm einen persönlichen Brief. Daher kommt von den drei Möglichkeiten nur „Hi Carlos," infrage.

b) Dear Ms Watson,
Hinweis: „Dear Sir/Madam," darfst du nicht verwenden, da du den Namen der Frau kennst. Da du nicht weißt, ob sie verheiratet ist oder nicht, schreibst du „Ms".

c) Dear Sir or Madam,
Hinweis: In Briefen an eine Person, deren Namen man nicht kennt, schreibt man „Dear Sir or Madam," bzw. „Dear Sir/Madam,".

d) Dear Granny,
Hinweis: An deine Großmutter schreibst du natürlich eine persönliche E-Mail. Von den angebotenen Optionen passt dazu nur „Dear Granny,".

Aufgabe 14

Hinweis: Auch für den passenden Abschluss von Briefen und E-Mails findest du die richtigen Wendungen in Kapitel 5.3. Es ist wieder ganz wichtig, zwischen Personen, die du gut kennst, und Adressaten eines offiziellen Schreibens zu unterscheiden. Analysiere also die Situationen in den Teilaufgaben a) bis d) sorgfältig, bevor du dich für eine Möglichkeit entscheidest.

a) Best wishes, Mike
Hinweis: Die beiden Brieffreunde kennen sich noch nicht so gut; um „Love" zu verwenden, müsstest du aber sicher sein, dass sich Carlos und Mike sehr nahestehen. „Yours sincerely," ist zu förmlich. „Best wishes," passt daher am besten.

b) Yours sincerely,
Hinweis: „Love," und „Best wishes," sind in einem Geschäftsbrief nicht angemessen.

c) Yours faithfully,
Hinweis: Wenn man den Adressaten nicht namentlich kennt, schreibt man in einem offiziellen Schreiben immer „Yours faithfully,".

d) Love,
Hinweis: Die einzig richtige Option für ein persönliches Schreiben ist hier „Love,".

Aufgabe 15

Hinweis: Überlege dir zuerst Vor- und Nachteile der beiden Möglichkeiten und sammle Ideen in einer Tabelle (Aufgabe a). Entscheide dich für die Möglichkeit, zu der dir Argumente einfallen, die du auch sicher auf Englisch ausdrücken kannst. Es ist nicht so wichtig, ob dies auch wirklich deiner Meinung entspricht. Beachte, dass du außerdem noch mindestens eine Aktivität vorschlagen sollst, die du während der Sprachreise unternehmen möchtest. Du kannst dich entweder von den Fotos inspirieren lassen oder andere Aktivitäten nennen.

a)

activities:	see Golden Gate Bridge, cable cars
advantages (sharing a flat):	would be fun, could cook together, spend free time together
advantages (host family):	hear correct English all day long, meet local people

preferred option:	host family (disadvantages of sharing a flat: you don't speak to local people, you also hear "bad English")

b) Hi Fabio,

I can't wait to set out on our adventure. One thing I really would like to see in San Francisco is the Golden Gate Bridge. (And a ride in one of those old-fashioned cable cars would also be great.) What about you?

I got the same e-mail about our accommodation in San Francisco. You've certainly got a point that staying somewhere together would be fantastic. You could teach me how to cook those delicious Italian pasta dishes that your mum cooked for us last summer.

Unfortunately my parents don't like the idea of us sharing a flat with other students – with no adults around to keep an eye on us. I think a host family might also be a good choice. Maybe there would be teenagers our age in the family and we could make friends. That way we would get to know locals who could show us the best places in the city. And of course a host family would also be better to improve our English. We'd hear (correct!) English all day long – and not just listen to other students' mistakes ;-). Why don't we ask to be placed in the same family or in two families in the same neighbourhood? What do you think?

Write soon,
(your name) *213 words*

Spezielle Übungen zu textgebundenen Schreibaufgaben

Allgemeiner Hinweis: In der MSA-Prüfung wird dir im Bereich „Schreiben" meist ein Text vorgelegt (z. B. ein Auszug aus einer Kurzgeschichte), auf den sich die Aufgaben beziehen. In einem ersten Schritt wird dabei überprüft, ob du den Text wirklich verstanden hast. Du wirst z. B. aufgefordert, den Text zusammenzufassen oder einen bestimmten Teilaspekt zu beschreiben. In einem zweiten Schritt musst du den Text dann genauer untersuchen bzw. interpretieren. Hier kann es sein, dass du bestimmte Zusammenhänge erklären musst, die Sprache analysieren oder einen Vergleich anstellen sollst. Die dritte Aufgabe geht meist über den Text hinaus – hier musst du zu einem Thema aus dem Text Stellung beziehen oder z. B. ein passendes Ende für die Geschichte schreiben.

Mit den folgenden Übungsaufgaben kannst du den Umgang mit solchen textgebundenen Schreibaufgaben gezielt trainieren. Die Übungen sollen dir ein Gefühl dafür vermitteln, was bei den verschiedenen Arbeitsaufträgen im Prüfungsteil „Schreiben“ („Sum up ...“, „Explain ...“, „Comment ...“ etc.) zu beachten ist.

Aufgabe 1

Hinweis: Diese Übung dient zur Vorbereitung auf Aufgaben mit der Anweisung „Sum up“. Eine wichtige Fertigkeit für das Schreiben von Zusammenfassungen besteht darin, Überbegriffe für die verschiedenen Teilaspekte eines Themas zu finden. Anstatt also alle im Text genannten Beispiele und Details eins-zu-eins wiederzugeben, musst du für ein „Summary“ Informationen sinnvoll bündeln können.

a)

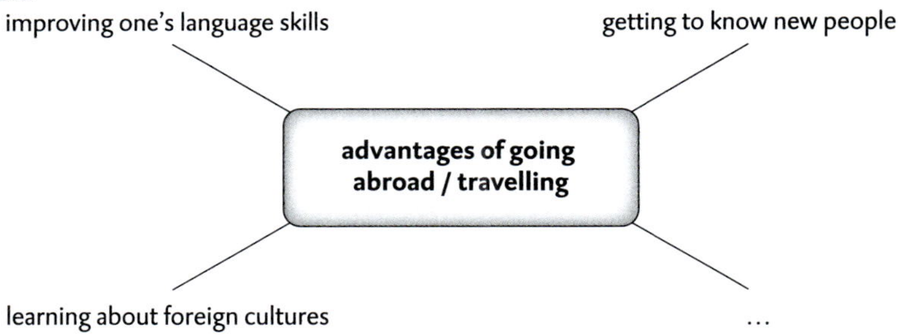

b)

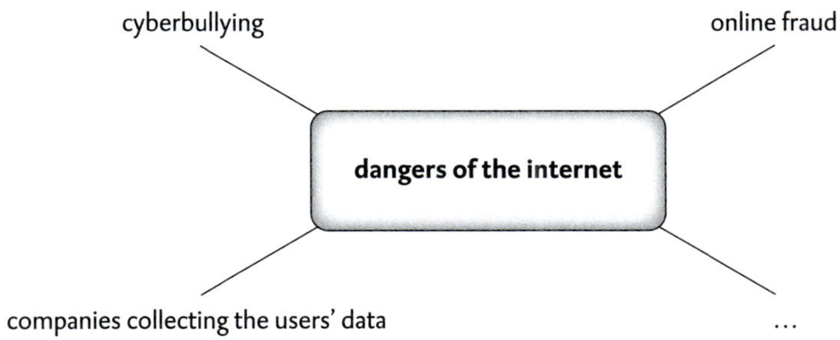

c)

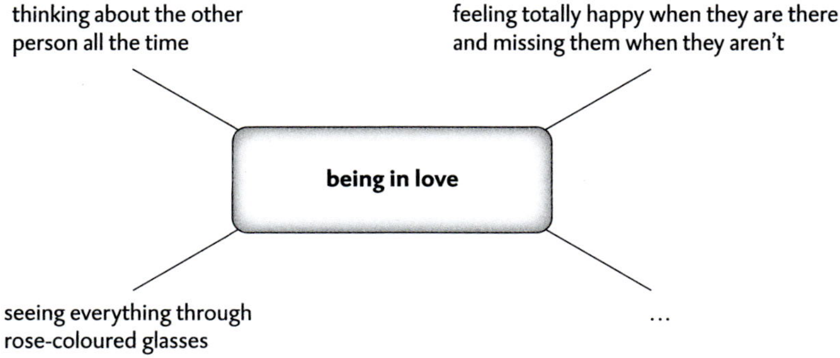

Aufgabe 2

Hinweis: Auch diese Aufgabe dient als Vorübung für die Aufgabenstellung „Sum up" bzw. „Summarise". Überlege, was die Funktion eines „Summarys" ist: Es dient dazu, jemandem, der einen Text noch nicht kennt, einen Überblick über die zentralen Inhalte zu vermitteln. Es empfiehlt sich also, zunächst den Autor/die Autorin, den Titel und (bei literarischen Texten) die Hauptfigur des Textes zu nennen. Als Nächstes sollte man die wichtigsten inhaltlichen Punkte knapp zusammenfassen. Mit unwichtigen Details oder einer reinen Nacherzählung der Geschichte würde man die andere Person vermutlich eher langweilen. Ebenso sollte man nicht versuchen, den Stil des Textes zu imitieren oder die eigene Meinung über den Text einfließen zu lassen. Das kann bei anderen Arbeitsaufträgen („Comment ...", „Write a suitable ending ...") verlangt sein, ist bei einem „Summary" aber nicht erwünscht.

- [x] the title and author of the text
- [ ] an exact re-telling of the story/text in chronological order
- [x] who the main character(s) is/are (if it is a literary text)
- [ ] your personal opinion on the text
- [ ] interesting dialogues
- [x] the main topic
- [ ] lots of details and examples
- [x] the most important aspects of the text "in a nutshell"
- [ ] phrases or sentences copied from the text

Aufgabe 3

Hinweis: Bei dieser Aufgabe sind zwei Beispiele für „Summaries" vorgegeben – ein negatives und ein positives. Du sollst jeweils überlegen, was daran nicht bzw. gut gelungen ist, und die entsprechenden Merkmale an den Rand schreiben. Wenn dir diese Übung noch schwerfällt, solltest du dir die Kennzeichen eines guten „Summarys" aus Aufgabe 2 noch einmal ins Gedächtnis rufen.

a)

Elliot was already in bed when his mother knocked on the door. "You've got to be patient with him, Elliot. He's ill. And we're going to have to accept that," said his mother. Elliot and his mother talked	beginning too abrupt: title / author / central topic not mentioned; direct speech
about his father. I think Elliot should be more understanding because it was not his father's fault that he was attacked.	personal opinion
The night that his father didn't come home, Elliot had already gone to bed. Half-asleep he heard the front door bell, unfamiliar voices, the door closing again, chairs scraping across the kitchen floor under his bedroom. Two policemen came into the room. The woman went back into the kitchen, and the man	chronological retelling of the story with lots of irrelevant details; phrases copied from the text
told the boy: "Can you go and get dressed?"	direct speech
Elliot and his mother visited his father in hospital.	
Elliot prayed, although he didn't believe in God.	irrelevant detail
That was three years ago. The bones had healed, his dad had come home, but it didn't get better. Finally,	
Elliot said to his mother: "I know it takes time, like the hospital said. I just wish – I just wish it had never happened, that's all."	direct speech

b)

The excerpt from the novel *Inventing Elliot* by Graham Gardner is about a boy, Elliot, and the relationship to his father, who was seriously injured in an attack and needs a long time to recover.	introduction mentioning the title / author / main character and central topic
A conversation with his mother one night leads Elliot to play over in his mind what happened. He thinks back to the time long before the accident, when he, his mum and his dad had spent lots of time together and were a happy family. He remembers how all that changed when his dad became increasingly busy with his work, and the shock he felt on the night of the attack: He almost couldn't believe it when the police told him that his dad had been attacked out of the blue and was lying seriously injured in hospital. Although Elliot's father was finally able to leave the hospital, he still suffers from depression and is not the same as before, a fact that seems hard for Elliot to accept.	summary of the most important elements of the story in own words

Text 1: The Double Life of Cassiel Roadnight

Aufgabe 2

Hinweis: Bei dieser Aufgabe sollst du selbst ein „Summary" schreiben. Formuliere zunächst eine kurze Einleitung, in der du den Titel des Romans, die Autorin, die Hauptfigur und das zentrale Thema nennst. Danach solltest du die wichtigsten Aspekte der Geschichte in deinen eigenen Worten zusammenfassen. Versuche jeweils, vom Text zu abstrahieren, d. h. ähnliche Aspekte unter einem Überbegriff oder in einem Satz zusammenzufassen anstatt die Geschichte in allen Einzelheiten nachzuerzählen.

The excerpt from *The Double Life of Cassiel Roadnight*, written by Jenny Valentine, deals with a boy who is mistaken for someone else and uses this unexpected chance to start a new life.
The unnamed narrator and main character is a homeless young man who goes to a hostel looking for food and shelter. When two members of the staff, Mr Gordon and a woman, talk to him, they suddenly discover that he looks very similar to a boy from a missing person's ad, a certain "Cassiel Roadnight". They are almost sure that the boy in front of them must be Cassiel and do not really believe the narrator when he says he is not. When the narrator becomes aware that Cassiel Roadnight has a family and friends who love him and that he might have the chance of finding a warm home away from the streets, he decides to pretend to be the missing boy and take on Cassiel's identity.

161 words

Aufgabe 3

Hinweis: Diese Aufgabe enthält die Arbeitsanweisung „Explain". Teilaufgabe a) dient nur zur Vorbereitung und soll dir helfen, zu verstehen, was genau bei diesem Aufgabentyp verlangt wird: Du sollst weder eine Zusammenfassung des Textes schreiben, noch deine eigene Meinung wiedergeben oder über den weiteren Handlungsverlauf spekulieren, sondern in einem sachlichen Stil bestimmte Textzusammenhänge erklären. In diesem Fall sollst du begründen, warum sich der Erzähler am Ende dazu entschließt, die Identität des vermissten Cassiel Roadnight anzunehmen. Lies dir den Text noch einmal im Hinblick auf die Aufgabenstellung durch, unterstreiche relevante Abschnitte und mache dir Notizen. An verschiedenen Stellen wird einerseits die derzeitige Lebenssituation des Erzählers beschrieben, z. B. dass er meist auf der Straße lebt, wenig zu essen und keine richtige Kleidung hat und dass sich niemand um ihn kümmert. Auf der anderen Seite schildert der Erzähler, wie er sich das Leben von Cassiel Roadnight vor dessen Verschwinden vorstellt: sorglos und in einem behüteten Zuhause bei liebevollen Menschen. Diese beiden Elemente musst du in deiner Lösung zu Teilaufgabe b) zusammenbringen und darlegen, dass sich der Erzähler durch seine Täuschung ein besseres Leben erhofft. Beachte, dass du deine Ausführungen durch konkrete Textbelege untermauern musst – du kannst dazu direkte Zitate oder indirekte Zeilenverweise (mit „cf.") verwenden.

a) ... give possible reasons for the protagonist's decision.
... support your findings with evidence from the text.

b) The narrator and protagonist of the story pretends to be Cassiel Roadnight because he hopes for a better life.
When he arrives at the shelter, the narrator is in a rather desperate situation. He is hungry and has no roof over his head – "half-starved" (l. 3), he is only looking for "two meals and a dry place to sleep" (ll. 7/8). Moreover, he appears to feel alone and without any perspective, which can be guessed from the fact that he says he is "nobody" (l. 15). By contrast, Cassiel Roadnight, the missing boy in the photo, appears to be free from worries. He is described as "happy and well fed and wholesome" (l. 43), with a "flawless, fearless face" (l. 59). The narrator concludes from the fact that Cassiel is being looked for that there must be people who love him and miss him (cf. l. 61). When the narrator is mistaken for Cassiel, he realises that this could be an unexpected way out of his situation: "He had a family and friends. He had loved ones. He had a life I could step right into. And what did I have? Nobody. Nothing." (ll. 62–64). Taking on Cassiel's identity enables him to leave his old life behind and start anew in a nice home, with friends and a family who care for him and a life full of opportunities. *230 words*

Text 2: The Art of Being Normal

Aufgabe 2

Hinweis: Auch diese Aufgabe enthält die Arbeitsanweisung „Explain". Du sollst hier erklären, warum sich Leo und Alicia so gut verstehen. Achte darauf, dass du nicht einfach den gesamten Romanauszug nacherzählst, sondern gezielt auf die möglichen Gründe eingehst. Gegen Mitte des Romanausschnitts findest du hierzu eine wichtige Information: Sowohl Leo als auch Alicia sind neu an die Schule gekommen und haben sich als Außenseiter gefühlt – Alicia kann also gut nachvollziehen, wie es Leo gerade geht, und Leo fühlt sich von Alicia verstanden.

Leo and Alicia seem to get on so well because they share the experience of being new at school and "different". Leo has only recently changed to Eden Park school. For some reason, most of the pupils are a bit afraid of him and keep their distance, treating him with a "mixture of fear and fascination, like [...] an exotic animal that may or may not be dangerous" (ll. 27–29). He is not invited to parties (cf. l. 26) and seems to feel rather insecure. When asked about Becky's party, for example, he pretends not to have heard about it, then nervously clears his throat (cf. l. 17) and later worries about having said something strange (cf. ll. 21–24). Alicia came to Eden Park in eighth form. As she was the only black girl then, she also knows what it means to be seen as "other": "Eden Park isn't the most diverse of schools. You can count the number of black kids here on two hands" (ll. 41/42). As a result, Alicia knows what Leo feels like and sympathises with his situation: "You know, I was the new kid once" (l. 34). However, she has made the experience that by actively seeking contact with the other pupils and taking part in group activities, one can break the ice and find friends (cf. ll. 45–48). By telling Leo her story and inviting him to come along to the party, she tries to give him hope that things will change for the better. Leo, in turn, is glad that Alicia talks to him without any fear or prejudice (cf. ll. 29/30) and that there is someone who understands his situation. *281 words*

Text 3: The OMG Blog

Aufgabe 2

Hinweis: Aufgaben mit dem Arbeitsauftrag „Comment" kommen relativ häufig in der Prüfung vor. Darin wird von dir verlangt, deine persönliche Meinung zu einem bestimmten Thema zu äußern. In diesem Fall musst du zu einem vorgegebenen Statement Stellung beziehen. In Teilaufgabe a) sollst du zunächst Argumente sammeln, die für oder gegen die Aussage sprechen. Im MSA wird zwar nicht ausdrücklich von dir verlangt, eine solche Tabelle anzulegen – dennoch kann dieses Vorgehen auch in der Prüfung nützlich sein. Deine Stichpunkte helfen dir, zu entscheiden, ob du der Aussage zustimmst, sie ablehnst oder eine Mittelposition einnimmst. Außerdem können dir deine Notizen bereits als grobe Gliederung für den Hauptteil deiner Stellungnahme dienen.
In Teilaufgabe b) sollst du deine Lösung dann ausformulieren. Beginne deine Stellungnahme mit einer kurzen Einleitung, in der du auf das Thema hinführst. Im Hauptteil legst du deine Position dar und begründest sie. Versuche jeweils, deine

Argumente mit konkreten Beispielen zu unterfüttern. Zum Schluss solltest du noch einmal ein persönliches Fazit ziehen.

a)

Arguments for	Arguments against
– children are too young to understand the possible dangers of the internet; examples: • their personal data might be misused • strangers might approach them • they might become addicted to the internet – conclusion: parents should teach their children how to use the internet safely	– children need access to the internet to develop skills in dealing with technology – children must have the chance to communicate online with friends, otherwise they might feel excluded

b) Most children growing up today can't imagine there ever was a world without the internet. Even very young children have a smartphone and go online every day. For parents, this raises the question if and to what degree they should control their children's online behaviour.

On the one hand, it is important that children get in contact with the internet at an early stage. Being able to deal with technology is a skill they need not only for school but also later in their working lives. What is more, most of the communication between young people happens via social media or messenger apps, where friends meet online to chat, play games etc. Parents shouldn't completely forbid their child to take part in these activities, as their son or daughter might soon lose touch with his or her friends or feel excluded. And especially for teenagers, there is nothing more annoying and embarrassing than overprotective parents!

On the other hand, it is also true that children are too young to understand the possible dangers of the internet. They often post private photos and give away very personal information on social networking sites without realising that this information is stored and might get into the wrong hands. They are not aware that the friendly stranger they are chatting with might not be another teenager, but a criminal adult who is trying to approach children. Lastly, because so much of their social life takes place on the web, children often spend many hours online and risk becoming addicted to the internet.

In conclusion, it is my opinion that parents should keep an eye on how much time their children spend online. They should also teach their children what to pay attention to when going on the internet, for example to be careful where and with whom they share personal information. In other words, parents should not control every single thing their children do on the internet, but rather teach their children to be safe online. And finally, parents need to be open to their child's problems and worries so that their son or daughter will turn to them if he/she is being bullied online.

361 words

Aufgabe 3

Hinweis: Auch bei dieser kreativen Schreibaufgabe sollst du vor dem eigentlichen Ausformulieren deiner Lösung zunächst Ideen, Beispiele und nützliche Wendungen sammeln. Als Gliederungspunkte dienen dafür die „prompts" aus der Aufgabenstellung. Ein solcher Zwischenschritt wird zwar in der Prüfung nicht ausdrücklich von dir verlangt, kann dir aber helfen, deine Lösung zu strukturieren und sicherzugehen, dass du keinen Aspekt vergisst.

a)

Aspects	Ideas/examples/useful phrases
a direct address to Zarah's mum:	**Dear mama2z**
a short summary of what happened and why Zarah is now angry with her mum:	• **I posted a video** • **you wrote a comment about it** • **now everyone is making fun of me, and I'm really embarrassed**
why she nevertheless loves her mum:	• **I know you mean well and only want to protect me** • **I appreciate that you care for me and are interested in my life**
a suggestion for what her mum and other parents could do better:	• **don't post comments that everyone can read** • **we can talk at home or you can write a text** • **allow us some freedom, don't treat us like babies!**

b) Dear mama2z,

Today I posted a really cool video of Blondie. But when I wanted to check whether my friends liked it too, I discovered that *you* had written a comment on it. Do you have any idea how embarrassing that is??!! If you wanted to say something about the video, you could have told me at home at the breakfast table, not online in front of all my friends and schoolmates. I'm so upset! Everyone's laughing at me – I don't even want to look into my Instagram account anymore because there are so many comments by people making fun of me.
I know you only meant well. I know you only want to protect me and that's why you're trying to check on what I'm doing online. And I know that you really care for me, for what interests me and who my friends are – and that's what I like about you.
But please, please – try to hold yourself back a little in the future. Don't try to act like you're my best friend, because that's really embarrassing. If you want to tell me something, we can talk at home or you can write me a text – you needn't write comments for the whole world to read. Will you promise me that?
And to all the other mums and dads out there who have stumbled across our blog – please try to do the same. Allow us some freedom and don't make us feel like babies (because we're not!), especially not in front of all our friends.

I love you, but – grrr!
Zarah *263 words*

Text 4: The Mystery of the Stolen FA Cup Medal

Aufgabe 2

Hinweis: Bei dieser Aufgabe musst du Davids Beziehung zu Fußball beschreiben. Lies den Text noch einmal durch und unterstreiche die Passagen, in denen es um Davids Verhältnis zum Fußball geht. So gehst du sicher, dass du nicht einfach die ganze Geschichte nacherzählst, sondern wirklich nur die für die Fragestellung relevanten Aspekte behandelst. Bei der Arbeitsanweisung „describe" ist es zudem wichtig, dass du neutral und sachlich formulierst, d. h., du darfst (anders als bei einem „Comment") nicht deine persönliche Meinung einfließen lassen.

a) ... sum up certain aspects of the story.

b) David is a passionate football fan – the sport obviously means a lot to him. But although he lives less than a mile from the stadium of his favourite club, Manchester United, he has never seen a live match there because he can't afford a ticket. Instead, he always listens to football matches on the radio and dreams of being in the stadium with the other fans, supporting his team.
David also regularly plays football in the garden by himself, trying to improve his technique. When he finds out that his next door neighbour is a former ManUtd player and that a football medal was stolen from his house, David immediately understands what a terrible loss this must mean for the man. *121 words*

Aufgabe 3

Hinweis: Bei dieser Aufgabe sollst du erklären, warum die Person, die den Ball über den Zaun zurückschießt, nichts zu David sagt. Dazu solltest du zunächst darauf eingehen, wer diese Person sein könnte. Da Davids Nachbar bereits zuvor mehrfach erwähnt wurde, liegt es nahe, dass er es sein könnte. Diese Vermutung bestätigt sich, als wir am Ende erfahren, dass er ein ehemaliger Fußballprofi ist – was erklärt, warum er David den Ball punktgenau zuspielt. Doch welche Gründe könnte er haben, nicht mit David zu reden? Wir wissen, dass er ein ehemaliger Fußballstar ist, der nun aber zurückgezogen in einer normalen Siedlung lebt und den niemand wirklich kennt. Vermutlich möchte der Mann unerkannt bleibt, um nicht die Aufmerksamkeit von Fans oder der Medien auf sich zu ziehen.

The person kicking the ball back over the fence is the former Manchester United player Arthur Stevens, the last surviving player of United's cup winning team of 1952 (cf. ll. 40–45). A superstar at the time, he now he lives in a normal neighbourhood not very far from his old workplace, the Manchester stadium (cf. l. 5). However, even people who live nearby, such as David, don't seem to know who the old man is: "David had never met his next door neighbour" (ll. 8/9). Moreover, he never leaves the house during the week (cf. ll. 11–13). It seems that after all the fame, Arthur Stevens just wants to enjoy the ordinary life of a retired man without being in the focus of the media and other people. That is probably why he does not say anything to David when he kicks the ball back over the fence. He does not want to give away who he is because that would probably mean the end to his quiet life – fans might gather around his house, the press might visit him etc. At the same time, he can't resist kicking the ball back and thus "communicating" with David without using words, perhaps because he feels the boy's passion for football and recognises his younger self in David. *218 words*

Aufgabe 4

Hinweis: Bei dieser Aufgabe sollst du untersuchen, wie in der Geschichte Spannung erzeugt wird. Du darfst also nicht einfach nur wiedergeben, was auf der Handlungsebene passiert, sondern musst auch darauf eingehen, wie die Geschichte erzählt wird (vgl. Teilaufgabe a).
*Lies dir den Text noch einmal durch und überlege, an welchen Stellen die Geschichte besonders spannend ist und woran das liegen könnte. Es kann z. B. damit zu tun haben, wann wir als Leser*innen bestimmte Informationen bekommen oder aus wessen Blickwinkel die Geschichte erzählt wird.*

a) ... also describe how the story is told.

b) The most important technique that is used to create suspense is that the reader is only given hints about what might happen – however, the decisive piece of information is left out or revealed relatively late. For example, in the first part of the story, we learn that David has been wondering for some time what kind of person his next door neighbour might be (cf. ll. 8–13). We can already guess from the fact that this is mentioned at all that the old man might become more important in the course of the story. However, we do not know yet what role he will play exactly and are therefore curious to find out.
The same technique is used when David kicks the ball over the fence. It is not said explicitly who kicks the ball back: "like a miracle, the ball came back, perfectly weighted to [David's] feet. [...] How had that happened?" (ll. 18/19). Instead, we are invited to draw our own conclusion that, perhaps, this might again have to do with the mysterious neighbour. It is only revealed towards the end of the excerpt that the old man is actually a former football star from Manchester United, and that someone broke into his house to steal his famous medal (cf. ll. 40–45). But again, it is mentioned relatively late that the burglar might have hidden the medal somewhere near the house (cf. l. 52), and so of course, the reader, again,

wants to know if it is still there … Another way of saying this is that we never know more than David does, which also makes it easier for us to identify with him.

279 words

Aufgabe 5

Hinweis: Bei dieser Aufgabe sollst du eine Fortsetzung der Geschichte schreiben – auch dieser Aufgabentyp kommt in der Prüfung relativ häufig vor. Eine Fortsetzung sollte sich möglichst nahtlos an den Ausgangstext anschließen. Dazu ist es u. a. wichtig, zunächst zu analysieren, in welchem Stil der Ausgangstext geschrieben ist. Wird er von einem Ich-Erzähler erzählt oder in der dritten Person? Wird als Zeitstufe das „present tense" oder „past tense" verwendet? Enthält der Text viele oder kaum/keine Dialoge? Diese Fragen aus Teilaufgabe a) werden zwar in der Prüfung nicht ausdrücklich abgefragt – dennoch solltest du dir vor dem Ausformulieren deiner Lösung kurz dazu Gedanken machen und ggf. Stichpunkte notieren. Auch mit Teilaufgabe b) kannst du trainieren, wie du in der Prüfung am besten vorgehst, nämlich indem du die „prompts" aus der Angabe als Grobgliederung verwendest und dir dazu Notizen machst.

a)

The story is told by …	
☐ a first-person narrator.	☑ a third-person narrator.
It is written in the …	
☐ simple present.	☑ simple past.
It includes …	
☐ both dialogues and narrated passages.	☑ hardly any dialogues.

b) *Beispiellösung:*

Aspects	Ideas/examples/useful phrases
what David does next:	He gets up and tries to find out if the medal is still there.
whether the medal is still there:	Yes, it is hidden behind a stone in the wall.
what happens the next time David sees the old man:	• David tells him the good news that the medal is still there.

	• The old man thanks David. • As a surprise, he invites him to come with him to the next Manchester United match.

c) David decided he had to find out. He slipped out of bed, took a torch and went out into the small alley behind Mr Steven's garden where he had seen the burglar. He searched the stone wall and tried to remember where the man had leaned against it. Suddenly, he discovered a stone that was only slightly sticking out. He pulled it out carefully and was blinded by the reflection of the torch light. The medal! David had to suppress a cry of joy. Mr Stevens would be so happy! He looked around to see if anyone had been watching him, then put the medal back in the wall and covered it with the stone. He didn't take it home because he didn't want anyone to think he had stolen it.

Back home, he lay in bed without sleeping, just waiting excitedly until the next morning. At seven, he decided it was okay to walk over to Mr Stevens. His hands became wet and shaky when he pressed the doorbell. Two long minutes later Mr Stevens opened the door: "Hello, young man. It's a bit early, don't you think?"

"Sorry sir, but I think I have good news for you." Mr Stevens asked David to come in and sit down. David was so excited – the words just came tumbling out of his mouth. After he had finished, they both went into the alley – luckily, the medal still was where David had found it the night before. Mr Stevens had tears in his eyes when he took it. "Thank you, David. This really means a lot to me."

A week later, David was waiting for the commentary of the Manchester United match against Arsenal on the radio when the doorbell rang. Mr Stevens stood outside. Behind him David saw a posh car.

"David, I'd like to invite you to come with me to the Old Trafford. Today is the match against Arsenal. If we win, we'll be champions. Would you like to join me?" David didn't know what to say. Half an hour later David sat in a VIP lounge at the Old Trafford next to Mr Stevens and other former Manchester players he knew from his football magazines.

David realised that this time it wasn't a dream, it was real. Manchester won the match against Arsenal 3:1 and became the new champion. In the evening the posh car brought David and Mr Stevens back home. In front of their houses, Mr Stevens told David that he should come over the next

day. Then he would tell him some stories of Manchester United, and probably they would play some football in the garden later.
Lying in bed later David thought that he was the luckiest boy on earth.

457 words

Text 5: Boot Camps for Teenagers

Aufgabe 2

Hinweis: Neben literarischen Texten können dir im Bereich „Schreiben“ in der Prüfung prinzipiell auch Sachtexte begegnen. Die Vorgehensweise beim Schreiben des „Summarys“ ist aber in beiden Fällen ähnlich: Nenne also zuerst den Titel des Textes und das zentrale Thema (der Name des Autors oder der Autorin ist hier nicht bekannt; eine Hauptfigur gibt es im Sachtext nicht). Gib dann die wichtigsten Punkte aus dem Text in deinen eigenen Worten wieder. Es hilft, wenn du dir zunächst die relevanten Stellen im Text unterstreichst und einige Notizen machst, bevor du mit dem Formulieren beginnst.

The text “Boot Camps for Teenagers” focuses on a particular way of dealing with young criminals. The so-called “boot camps” were introduced in the United States in the 1980s. They are based on military training camps and are seen as a balance between the options of probation (which is seen as not strict enough) and a prison sentence. The ideas behind boot camps are deterrence, reducing the number of prisoners, lowering costs and reducing recidivism among young criminals. Boot camps exist in over 30 US states, but are now forbidden in some. Many camps now also offer other services for the young criminals, apart from simply punishing them. Despite these efforts, the boot camp system has many critics, and has been rejected by experts in many European countries and in Canada.

131 words

Aufgabe 3

Hinweis: Bei dieser Aufgabe sollst du erklären, warum Bootcamps von vielen Menschen kritisch gesehen werden. Gehe dazu den Text noch einmal durch und markiere dir die Stellen, an denen Kritik an den Bootcamps erwähnt wird. Auf diese Weise stellst du sicher, dass deine Lösung wirklich nur die für die Aufgabe relevanten Informationen enthält. Überlege als Nächstes, in welcher Reihenfolge du die verschiedenen Aspekte erwähnen könntest, damit ein möglichst schlüssiger

Text entsteht. Jetzt kannst du mit dem Ausformulieren deiner Lösung beginnen. Achte darauf, nicht einfach aus dem Text abzuschreiben, sondern eigene Formulierungen zu verwenden. Versuche, deine Sätze logisch miteinander zu verknüpfen. Das erreichst du z. B. durch sogenannte „linking words" (z. B. „in addition", „as a result" etc.).

According to the text, the general experience of a sentence in a US boot camp for young criminals is one of punishment and extreme conditions: "The methods can be seen as 'shock treatment': military-style training and marching" (ll. 35–37). The criminals get no motivation or encouragement, but only criticism and punishment (cf. ll. 16–18). There have been cases of deaths in boot camps, and as a result the boot camp system no longer exists in Florida (cf. ll. 45–51). The whole system is based on youths submitting to superiors: "The idea was to break a person down and then rebuild them with the 'correct' behaviour" (ll. 19–21). In general it can be stated that the aims of boot camps – deterrence and a lower rate of recidivism – have never been reached (cf. ll. 61–63). It cannot be proven whether young people are scared of boot camp and therefore stay away from crime (cf. ll. 69–72). In addition, boot camps have not been successful in reducing the number of criminals who get involved in crime again after completing a sentence: "youths coming out of a boot camp are just as likely to return to crime as those coming out of prison" (ll. 65–68). The system is even accused of bringing out exactly the types of behaviour that may cause young people to turn to crime: "such a system fixated on obedience and strict rules will develop frustration, a feeling of inferiority and, of course, aggression" (ll. 80–83). So instead of helping youths to cope with difficult emotions, the boot camp system makes these feelings worse.

271 words

Aufgabe 4

Hinweis: Beachte folgende Regeln, wenn du einen Tagebucheintrag verfassen sollst: Wie bei jeder kreativen Schreibaufgabe solltest du dir zuerst genau ansehen, aus wessen Sicht der Text geschrieben werden soll. Der Tagebucheintrag muss zum Charakter dieser Person passen. Du kannst einen solchen Text mit „Dear diary," beginnen oder auch einfach mit der Angabe eines Datums. Tagebucheinträge werden in der Ich-Form geschrieben. Da sie eigentlich nicht dazu bestimmt sind, von anderen gelesen zu werden, kann sich der Verfasser oder die Verfasserin frei über persönliche Gedanken und Gefühle äußern. Daher gibt es auch keine strengen Vorgaben über den sprachlichen Stil des Textes – er muss aber zu der Person passen, die das Tagebuch schreibt.

June 24

I've been here for three weeks now, and I've finally got used to the work. This is the first evening when I'm not too exhausted to write anything in my diary. Today was the same as every other day: hard physical exercise outside, being shouted at in classrooms, horrible food (never enough, we're hungry all the time) and no time to relax.
The drill instructors are all like something out of a bad war film and they shout and push us all day long. You only have to be a few seconds slower than the fastest person in a race, or to get one answer wrong in a test, and you immediately have to run for miles with a 40-pound rucksack on your back, or stand up in class and explain why you're so stupid.
It seems like everything here is about pain and punishment and making people feel horrible – I don't know what the point is. If I went to prison, I'd have lots of time to sit around, bored, and think about what I've done, what I could have done better, and what I'll do differently in future. But here, there's no time to think about anything. All that most of us seem to learn is that we hate our superiors and being told what to do. I can see that if I was a soldier, this would be good training for me. But I don't want to join the army. I go to bed every night and dream about beating up the drill instructors, and then getting out of here and making sure that no one else ever tells me what to do, ever again. That can't really be the point of this, can it? *290 words*

Text 6: Sundae Girl

Hinweis: Diese Aufgabe solltest du unter Prüfungsbedingungen bearbeiten, um dich an den Zeitdruck zu gewöhnen. In den vorigen Aufgaben hast du bereits trainiert, wie man an die Aufgaben im Prüfungsteil „Schreiben" herangeht: Analysiere bei jeder Aufgabe als erstes, welcher Arbeitsauftrag vorliegt. Unterstreiche dann die für die Aufgabe relevanten Stellen im Ausgangstext und/oder mache dir Notizen. Strukturiere deine Notizen, um eine grobe Gliederung für deine Antwort zu erhalten, und überprüfe noch einmal, ob du alle in der Aufgabenstellung genannten Aspekte berücksichtigt hast. Beginne dann mit dem Ausformulieren deiner Lösung. Ganz zum Schluss solltest du deinen Text noch einmal im Hinblick auf Rechtschreib- oder Grammatikfehler kontrollieren.

Aufgabe 2

Jude, the narrator of Cathy Cassidy's novel *Sundae Girl*, seems to have a rather "unconventional" family. Her mother now works as a hairdresser but is very proud of her past as a musical star. Jude's father is in "show business", too. He works as an Elvis Presley impersonator; in other words, he dresses up like Elvis, wears his hair like Elvis, and sings Elvis songs in front of a (rather small) audience. Jude's grandparents also dress and behave unusually: Her grandfather, for example, wears a Marilyn Monroe tie, and her grandmother is knitting a (3 meter long) scarf during Parents' Night. *101 words*

Aufgabe 3

When Kevin Carter asks Jude about the two elderly people at Parents' Night, the narrator pretends that they are not her own grandparents but Kristina Kowalski's mum and dad. The reason for this is that Jude is rather ashamed of her family: "I'm [...] anxious that school will find out the truth about my family. And now they are here for Parents' Night – all of them. Nightmare." (ll. 7–9) She finds the way her grandparents and parents behave embarrassing and does not want to be connected with them. That is why she "hiss[es]" (l. 22) when her mother begins to talk about her musical past, pretends that she doesn't know who the person in the Elvis costume is (cf. ll. 43–47) and also distances herself from her grandparents. Jude lies about her family because she does not want to be regarded as uncool and as a "poor kid" (ll. 59, 60/61) by her classmate Kevin. At the same time, the lie about her grandparents also allows Jude to put Kristina Kowalski in a negative light. Kevin finds Kristina attractive (cf. l. 51), but Jude does not really like her and even seems a bit jealous of her. *199 words*

Aufgabe 4

a) I guess we all remember situations when our parents, siblings or other relatives really got on our nerves. In moments like these, the saying "one cannot choose one's family" may have crossed your mind. But is this statement actually true?

On the one hand, it is right, of course: You are born into a certain family and have to deal with this fact, at least for the next 18 (or so) years. As a young person especially, it is often frustrating to be dependent on adults whom you find too strict or – like the narrator of *Sundae Girl* – really embarrassing. Mostly, however, the conflicts with your parents are forgotten after a few days, and you are quite happy to live with the people who know you the best and who love you.

However, for some people, the relationship to their families remains very difficult. At least when you are grown up (and to some extent also earlier), you can always find friends or a partner who will love you and accept you just the way you are. Perhaps not biologically, but socially, those people can become something like a new or additional family.

In conclusion, I therefore believe that the above saying is not entirely true and that it is actually possible to choose one's family. *216 words*

b) Just as the words have left my mouth, Gran suddenly looks up from her scarf and starts waving at me. "Huhu, Jude, dear, why didn't you tell us you were here?" As they're moving over to us, I feel my face turning bright red. Kevin Carter looks at me questioningly.

"Oh ... hi, Grandma ... hi, Grandpa ...," I mutter. "Sorry, I didn't see you." Kevin's mouth is still standing open. "Em ... nice tie!" is all he can manage.

"That boy's got taste!" Grandad says, looking really pleased. "Are you Jude's boyfriend? You know, Granny and me have been wondering when she would ever start dating somebody ..."

Ground, open up ...

Kevin still looks a bit perplexed, but then he says confidently, "Yes! In fact, I am." I stare at him. "Although we haven't been together very long," he winks at me.

I still don't know if I heard correctly and my mouth is too dry to speak. But suddenly I'm thinking that maybe the evening isn't so bad after all.

173 words

▶ Lösungen zu den Original-Aufgaben der zentralen Prüfung in NRW

Erster Prüfungsteil: Hörverstehen

Hörverstehen Teil 1: *Lighthouse Walk*

1. c) … take photographs.
   Hinweis: "… take nothing but pictures …" (Z. 11)

2. a) … the cliffs.
   Hinweis: "That's why you can see them sitting along the rocky areas, eating straight off the rocks." (Z. 17/18)

3. a) … against the law.
   Hinweis: "Feeding baboons is illegal in any national park." (Z. 19)

4. a) … during bad weather.
   Hinweis: "Legend says that a terrible storm hit the ship." (Z. 27)

5. c) … still travel the oceans.
   Hinweis: "And this is why they have to sail the seas forever as ghosts." (Z. 31)

6. a) … rough sea.
   Hinweis: "The waters here are quite wild and strong storms often hit the coast." (Z. 33/34)

7. c) … stormy weather.
   Hinweis: "The wind up here is very strong and it could blow you right off the cliff." (Z. 42/43)

8. b) … in the wrong place.
   Hinweis: "You would think this would be the perfect location for a lighthouse, but actually it's too high! That's why the light is often hidden by fog." (Z. 46–48)

9. b) … was finished in 1919.
   Hinweis: "It was completed in 1919 …" (Z. 50)

Hörverstehen Teil 2: #*YourChoice*

1. c) … African hairstyles.
   Hinweis: "What actually happened is that our school rules banned all Afro hair fashion like rasta hairstyle, braids and dreadlocks last month." (Z. 11/12)

2. c) … cultural identity.
   Hinweis: "This is Africa, and we can't be naturally who we are?" (Z. 16)

3. b) … an educational trend.
   Hinweis: "Many South African schools have introduced similar rules before." (Z. 22/23)

4. a) … stopped the rule.
   Hinweis: "Our school dropped the restrictions a few days later …" (Z. 24)

5. a) … Internet protests.
   Hinweis: "… thousands of people signed an online petition supporting our protest." (Z. 26/27)

6. c) … the learners' concentration.
   Hinweis: "Some South African teachers argue that the reason for hair and dress codes is that personal expression can take the focus away from learning." (Z. 31/32)

7. b) … exclusion from school.
   Hinweis: "Those who didn't stick to the rule were told to cut their hair or else be banned from school." (Z. 38/39)

8. c) … media report.
   Hinweis: "That's why she has decided to work on a documentary about hair and black identity that will be released next year." (Z. 45/46)

9. c) … discriminating.
   Hinweis: "And the education minister even ordered an investigation because some people said that the school rule was racist." (Z. 47/48)

Zweiter Prüfungsteil: Leseverstehen – Wortschatz – Schreiben

Leseverstehen: *Please, Sir – sit! The story of a learning support dog*

1. true
   Evidence: staff managed to solve the problem pretty much overnight [. . .] by employing [. . .] Rolo, the school dog. / Within a week of 'Operation Rolo Says No', the school grounds were spotless
   ✐ *Hinweis: Z. 2–5 und Z. 12/13*

2. c) . . . made them feel badly about their behaviour.
   Evidence: This clever tactic of emotional blackmail pictured the five-month-old, chocolate-brown Labrador.
   ✐ *Hinweis: Z. 8–10*

3. true
   Evidence: the 1,500 students had worked together to clean it up
   ✐ *Hinweis: Z. 13/14*

4. a) . . . indicated by a notice.
   Evidence: a sign [. . .] shows when the puppy is at school
   ✐ *Hinweis: Z. 15–17*

5. false
   Evidence: He has his own name tag, 'Mr Rolo', just like any other member of the staff.
   ✐ *Hinweis: Z. 19/20*

6. a) . . . a recent trend in the UK.
   Evidence: a phenomenon which can be found more and more in modern classrooms / "In the last two or three years the number of dogs in schools has exploded in a really big way"
   ✐ *Hinweis: Z. 21/22 und Z. 23/24*

7. a) … the dogs' well-being.
Evidence: too many dogs are unprepared for classroom life and have no proper training / "It is not right for all dogs" / "There are probably hundreds and hundreds of dogs in schools […], many not properly trained."
Hinweis: Z. 26–28

8. false
Evidence: The *Department for Education* has no idea how many dogs are currently working in classrooms and does not require schools to register […] their animals.
Hinweis: Z. 29/30

9. true
Evidence: Classroom dogs […] have a calming effect /
"[…] the children don't want to wake him so they are really quiet"
Hinweis: Z. 31/32 und Z. 34/35

10. c) … believe in their abilities.
Evidence: help children read aloud more confidently / encouraging them to turn a page
Hinweis: Z. 36/37 und Z. 38

Wortschatz: *The British school system*

1. b) … divided into …
2. attend / go to /…
3. d) … mixed, …
4. a) … abilities …
5. c) … selective …
6. exam / entrance exam / test / entry test / admission test /…
7. take / pass / do / sit / gain / achieve /…
8. a) … identity.
9. rules / regulations / requirements / guidelines / restrictions /…
10. b) … run from …

11. get / receive / find / ask for /…

12. activities / extra-curricular activities / options /…

13. d) … participate in.

14. compulsory / obligatory / a must /…

Schreiben: *Jessica's speech*

✎ *Hinweis: Der Prüfungsteil „Schreiben" besteht in der Regel aus drei Aufgaben. Mit der ersten Aufgabe soll geprüft werden, ob du den Text wirklich verstanden hast. Bei der zweiten Aufgabe musst du den Text interpretieren und dabei auch Textbelege anführen, um deine Untersuchungsergebnisse zu untermauern. Im dritten Teil hast du die Wahl zwischen einer persönlichen Stellungnahme und einer kreativen Aufgabe. Am besten entscheidest du dich für das Thema (3a oder 3b), zu dem dir spontan am meisten einfällt und das du sprachlich am besten bewältigen kannst.*

1. ✎ *Hinweis: Bei dieser Aufgabe sollst du zusammenfassen, was du im Text über Jessicas Leben und die politische Situation in Südafrika erfährst. Lies dir die Erzählung noch einmal durch und markiere alle Stellen, an denen etwas zu diesen beiden Themen gesagt wird. Versuche dann, die wichtigsten Informationen knapp und in deinen eigenen Worten wiederzugeben.*

Jessica is a 15-year-old white girl from Cape Town. Her parents have sent her to live with her grandmother in London because there is a lot of violence in South Africa in the early 1990s. In her home country, Jessica has a black friend named Daisy and a white boyfriend called Ben. At the moment Jessica doesn't know where Daisy is because she has to hide from the South African police, and her boyfriend Ben is in prison. Their crime is that they have actively opposed the apartheid regime.

Apartheid means racial segregation in all areas of public life. A lot of places are for whites only, and black and white pupils are not in the same class. It also means social inequality. For example, Jessica's home in South Africa is in a wealthy suburb, while Daisy lives in a poor township. Moreover, people who support the anti-apartheid movement are persecuted and put into prison. *155 words*

2. *Hinweis: Gehe den Text noch einmal durch. Streiche dabei alle Stellen an, an denen Jessicas Verhaltensweisen und Gefühle beschrieben werden (etwa, als sie erfährt, dass sie eine Rede halten soll) oder an denen sie von ihren Freunden Daisy und Ben spricht. Überlege jeweils, was dir diese Stellen über Jessicas Charakter verraten: Welche Art von Mensch ist sie und was ist ihr wichtig? Versuche, passende Überbegriffe oder Beschreibungen zu finden (z. B. „rather shy", „friendship is very important"). In deiner Lösung kannst du entweder zuerst Jessicas Verhaltensweisen beschreiben und daraus bestimmte Wesenszüge ableiten oder du erwähnst gleich, welche Charaktereigenschaften sie hat, und untermauerst deine Beobachtung dann mit konkreten Beispielen.*

   At first, Jessica appears to be a rather shy girl. For example, she worries about why she is called to the principal's office (cf. ll. 2–4) and looks like a "frightened rabbit" (l. 8) once she has arrived there. When Mr Herbert suggests that she should talk about the situation in South Africa at the assembly, she is scared because she doesn't know what to say: "I'd never done anything like it in my life." (l. 15) But then she thinks of her friend Daisy and her boyfriend Ben and decides to give the speech for them (cf. ll. 15–17). This shows that her friends are very important to her and that she can overcome her shyness in order to help them.

   In her speech, Jessica talks in a very emotional way about the difficult situation Ben and Daisy are in: "One of the hardest things about leaving South Africa was leaving my best friend, Daisy, and the love of my life, Ben. We didn't even get the chance to say goodbye. He's in prison, in solitary confinement which means he's all alone in a very small and empty cell." (ll. 24–27) She tries to convince the other pupils to support the boycott of South African products as a protest against apartheid (cf. ll. 42–47). Jessica seems to have a strong sense of justice and wants to use her speech to support black people in South Africa. The shy schoolgirl has become a self-confident anti-apartheid activist. *250 words*

3. a) *Hinweis: Bei dieser Aufgabe sollst du begründen, warum der Titel von Babette Browns Buch,* Separation, *zu dem vorliegenden Textausschnitt passt. Durch die Leitfragen in der Aufgabenstellung ist bereits eine grobe Gliederung für deine Lösung vorgegeben: Du solltest also zunächst anführen, wer im Text von wem getrennt wird. Als nächstes musst du erklären, warum diese Personen voneinander getrennt werden – hier ist es wichtig, dass du auf die Apartheid (das politische System der Rassentrennung in*

Südafrika) eingehst. Zuletzt sollst du darlegen, warum sich die Autorin deiner Meinung nach für den Titel Separation *entschieden haben könnte.*

I think the title of Babette Brown's book, *Separation,* fits very well because being separated plays an important role in the text.
Jessica is sent to London because of the violent situation in South Africa. This means separation from her home country, her parents, her best friend Daisy and her beloved boyfriend Ben. As Daisy had to go into hiding and Ben is in prison, there is no contact between the three – all relationships have been cut off. But even while Jessica was still in South Africa, she and Daisy were often separated because they could not go to the same places or travel on the same bus. They also lived in separate neighbourhoods – Daisy in a poor township and Jessica and Ben in a rich white suburb.
All these separations have to do with the system of apartheid in South Africa. Until the early 1990s, black and white people were racially segregated. For example, lots of beaches, benches or cinemas were for whites only. White South Africans enjoyed a comfortable life, while non-white people had to live in poverty and were oppressed. People who rebelled against that injustice (such as Daisy and Ben in the story) were put into prison or risked their lives.
I think with the title *Separation*, Babette Brown wants to point to the pain connected with apartheid. Friendships between people with different skin colours were torn apart. Even some white people were separated from white people, like Jessica from her parents and her boyfriend. Apartheid meant suffering for nearly everybody. *255 words*

b) *Hinweis: Bei dieser Aufgabe sollst du eine Fortsetzung für den Text schreiben. Du sollst schildern, wie die Jungen und Mädchen aus Jessicas Klasse nach ihrer Rede reagieren, welche Ideen sie haben, um auf das Apartheidsystem aufmerksam zu machen und etwas dagegen zu unternehmen, und wie Jessica die Situation erlebt. Achte darauf, dass wirklich alle vier Aspekte in deiner Lösung enthalten sind. In der Aufgabenstellung ist außerdem vorgegeben, mit welchen Wörtern deine Fortsetzung beginnen soll. Das ist auch als Hilfestellung gedacht, damit du für deinen Text gleich die richtige Perspektive und Zeitform wählst (Ich-Perspektive und „simple past").*

I was really surprised – everybody seemed shocked about what I had told them. All my classmates gathered around me, asked questions and tried to comfort me.
"Poor Jessica, we had no clue about your life in South Africa," Lisa started.
"And your boyfriend is in prison? How long does he have to stay there?" Michael asked.
"Well, actually I don't really know. It depends on the government and how long they're going to keep their apartheid policy," I said. "I can't stop thinking of my parents, Daisy and of course Ben. I miss them all so much …" Suddenly, tears came to my eyes.
Lisa took me in her arms. "Don't cry, Jessica. We'll help you and your friends."
"Yes, we will!" the others nodded.
"Before you told us, I had no idea about how bad the situation was. I think everyone should know about how cruel the system is," Jake said. "Maybe we could organise a demonstration and paint posters or hand out leaflets."
"Yeah, and we could write an article for the local newspaper and see if they'll publish it. What do you think, Jessica?"
I almost found myself speechless because I was so overwhelmed by their support. "That would be fantastic …"
"And of course we have to tell everyone in our family that they should boycott products from South Africa. This will put pressure on the government to stop their apartheid policy," Bethany added.
We planned a meeting for the next day to prepare the demonstrations and work on our article. Then we went to see Mr Herbert to inform him about our plans.
When I walked home from school that day with Lisa, I was still moved by my classmates' reactions.
"All of you have been so helpful today. You are really good friends!"
"No problem, Jessica. You're not alone. We'll help Ben and Daisy. Tomorrow we'll start our initiative. We'll show the South African government what we think about apartheid."
I looked into her eyes and smiled: "Yeah, tomorrow we'll start! Tomorrow, we'll do it!" *336 words*

Erster Prüfungsteil: Hörverstehen

Hörverstehen Teil 1: *The summer plans of Danny Boyle*

1. b) … go on a trip to Ireland.
   Hinweis: "Danny Boyle sat in his room with a map of Ireland lying on his bed. He was carefully circling all the destinations where he and his family would be going on their summer vacation." (Z. 1–3)

2. b) … other countries.
   Hinweis: "Danny loved to read about distant locations …" (Z. 6)

3. c) … adventurous.
   Hinweis: "Not much happened in Rivertown, so Danny was always looking for adventure wherever he could find it." (Z. 10/11)

4. b) … in his school year.
   Hinweis: "Even though Danny was two years older than Melinda, they were in the same grade. This fact annoyed Danny …" (Z. 14–16)

5. c) … disinterest.
   Hinweis: "'Go away,' Danny said, keeping his eyes on the map. 'Don't you want to know what I've been doing?' 'Does it look like it?'" (Z. 20–22)

6. b) … know-it-all.
   Hinweis: Melinda verhält sich ziemlich besserwisserisch. Sie prahlt mit ihren Sprachkenntnissen (vgl. Z. 23–27) und tut so, als wüsste Danny nicht, dass es keine Feen gibt und was eine Legende sei (vgl. Z. 28/29).

7. b) … strange locations.
   Hinweis: "But there are some dark and mysterious places in Ireland that I want to explore." (Z. 31/32)

8. c) … continue his earlier activity.
   Hinweis: "Now can I go back to what I was doing?" (Z. 35)

9. a) … bad weather.
   Hinweis: "Even though it was summer, Ireland can be cool and wet …" (Z. 38/39)

10. c) … nightmare.
Hinweis: "He dreamed that he was alone on a windy island surrounded by fireballs that were leading him to the edge of a cliff. He then began falling down towards the ocean below." (Z. 41–43)

Hörverstehen Teil 2: *Thomas Caffrey's chocolate world*

1. a) … an unhappy event.
Hinweis: "Sad news for the children of Ireland and chocolate lovers everywhere: Dublin's favourite chocolate creator, the legendary Thomas Caffrey, died yesterday." (Z. 2–4)

2. b) … close relatives.
Hinweis: "We have Neville Caffrey, who is Thomas Caffrey's son, on the line." (Z. 5/6)

3. a) … family affair.
Hinweis: "Your business is now in its third generation." (Z. 9)

4. a) … holiday job.
Hinweis: "During summers as a little boy he worked in the chocolate factory of his brother William." (Z. 16/17)

5. c) … business deal.
Hinweis: "His great breakthrough came when he got a contract with a huge chain of shops in the 1950s." (Z. 21/22)

6. c) … one of Caffrey's creations in particular.
Hinweis: "Among the many of Caffrey's creations are Ireland's all time favourite, the Chocolate Snowball." (Z. 24/25)

7. c) … child's plaything.
Hinweis: "I remember when I was little I was on the floor with my little toy mouse, and my dad picked it up and said, 'Can I borrow this?' He went away with it 30 and used it as a model for his Marshmallow Mice." (Z. 27–30)

8. c) … has completely disappeared.
Hinweis: "The Marshmallow Mice are no longer sold." (Z. 34)

9. b) … big hearted.
   ✎ *Hinweis: "I remember as a kid I used to go to the company and my father, who was a very fine man, used to give a few sweets to me, and my brothers and sisters and to other kids." (Z. 38–40)*

10. b) … in some countries.
   ✎ *Hinweis: "You can also buy our products in Australia, Canada and in the United States." (Z. 43/44)*

Zweiter Prüfungsteil: Leseverstehen – Wortschatz – Schreiben

Leseverstehen: *The family that is enough*

1. false
   Evidence: Colfer, the second of five boys
   ✎ *Hinweis: Z. 3*

2. a) … family.
   Evidence: His relationship with his brothers […] explains the quick, dry humour in his books. / when Eoin started to write books, his brothers became the characters. / All five boys are part of the story. / Colfer's kids have changed his writing.
   ✎ *Hinweis: Z. 5–7, Z. 20–21, Z. 35*

3. c) … lots of fantastic tales.
   Evidence: my dad would tell us all stories about fairies and dragons
   ✎ *Hinweis: Z. 13/14*

4. false
   Evidence: Eoin […] invented his own characters and drew and wrote his own comics / His interest in writing continued as a love of drama / He […] learned her lines with her and had parts in Wexford Opera Festival productions.
   ✎ *Hinweis: Z. 16–19*

5. true
   Evidence: his brothers became the characters. / All five boys are part of the story. / Their names are almost identical to those of Eoin's brothers.
   ✎ *Hinweis: Z. 20–23*

6. b) … already had some experience in the job.
   Evidence: Eoin had written three other children's books
   ✎ *Hinweis: Z. 24*

7. false
   Evidence: The money was not as big as has been reported, but fame came fast and bigger money followed later.
   ✎ *Hinweis: Z. 30/31*

8. c) … behaved like they had before.
   Evidence: "Not as much as you would expect," / people in Wexford aren't interested in wealth and fame: "They've known me for decades, so they don't care."
   ✎ *Hinweis: Z. 31–34*

9. true
   Evidence: Didn't that change things? "Not as much as you would expect," says Eoin. / The brothers keep his feet on the ground too
   ✎ *Hinweis: Z. 31/32, Z. 34*

10. true
    Evidence: Colfer's kids have changed his writing. / "He comes up with some great funny remarks and I get a lot of material straight from him." / When Finn argues in the back of the car, Eoin […] tries to remember it for his books.
    ✎ *Hinweis: Z. 35–39*

11. a) … gentler.
    Evidence: The realisation that his children would one day read his books also made him think about the violence. / "There is a huge fight in the first book. I decided there was no need for that really … Now there are struggles but not much actual violence."
    ✎ *Hinweis: Z. 40–43*

12. b) … nice.
    Evidence: "Once he turns completely good, that's it."
    Hinweis: Z. 46/47

Wortschatz: *Welcome to "Thinkuknow"*

1. share / post / upload / put / publish / …
2. c) … digital …
3. private / secret / hidden / to ourselves /…
4. d) … sharing …
5. … spread / send / give / forward /pass on / communicate /…
6. a) … control …
7. fake / false / made-up / invented /…
8. a) … give away.
9. talk / write / have contact /…
10. dangerous / risky / a danger / a risk / unsafe /…
11. c) … account.
12. b) … block …
13. message / mail / text message / note /…

Schreiben: *Click'd*

Hinweis: Im Bereich „Schreiben" musst du drei Aufgaben zu einem Text bearbeiten. Lies dir zunächst den Text einmal gründlich durch. Sieh dir anschließend die Aufgaben dazu an. In Aufgabe 1 wird geprüft, ob du den Text verstanden hast. In Aufgabe 2 musst du dich dann detaillierter mit dem Text auseinandersetzen. Wichtig ist dabei, dass du Strategien der Textarbeit, die ihr im Unterricht besprochen habt, nutzt. Mache dir Notizen, verwende konkrete Textbelege und baue sie sinnvoll in deine Lösung ein. Achte dabei auf die richtige Zitierweise. Bei Aufgabe 3 hast du die Wahl zwischen mehreren Themen – in diesem Fall einer persönlichen Stellungnahme (Teilaufgabe a), einem Artikel (Teilaufgabe b) und einer Rede (Teilaufgabe c). Überlege dir, zu welcher Aufgabenstellung dir spontan am meisten einfällt und welche Textsorte dir am besten liegt. Entscheide dich dann für eine Teilaufgabe und konzentriere dich ausschließlich darauf. Vermeide also wenn möglich, zwischendurch noch einmal das Thema zu wechseln, da dich das wertvolle Zeit kostet.

1. *Hinweis: Bei dieser Aufgabe musst du auf drei Aspekte eingehen: Du sollst beschreiben, welches Produkt Allie entwickelt hat, wie es funktioniert und warum sie es erfunden hat. Überfliege den Text noch einmal und unterstreiche die Stellen, an denen du Informationen zu diesen drei Aspekten findest. Mache dir ggf. Notizen am Rand und formuliere dann deine Lösung in eigenen Worten aus.*

   Allie has invented a mobile app during her stay in a special camp on computers, the Code Girls Camp. It is called *Click'd*. — Allie's product

   The app uses quiz questions to collect personal information about its users, find out what people have in common and bring people with similar interests together. — how it works

   Allie got the idea for *Click'd* at the beginning of the camp. When she arrived, she didn't know any of the other girls and wasn't sure how to get to know them. With her invention, she wanted to find a way for people to get in touch with each other more easily. *101 words* — why she has created it

2. *Hinweis: Bei dieser Aufgabe sollst du erklären, wie sich Allies Gefühle während der Präsentation ihrer App verändern. Lies dir den Text noch einmal genau durch und unterstreiche alle Stellen, an denen beschrieben wird, wie Allie spricht und sich auf der Bühne bewegt. Daraus kannst du schließen, wie sie sich in der Situation fühlt. Versuche jeweils, passende Adjektive für ihre Gefühle zu finden (z. B. „nervous", „self-confident") und notiere sie dir am Rand. Beim Ausformulieren deiner Lösung solltest du Allies Gefühle immer zunächst in eigenen Worten beschreiben (dazu kannst du auf deine Notizen zurückgreifen) und anschließend ein konkretes Textbeispiel dazu geben (hier helfen dir die Unterstreichungen). Du kannst entweder ein wörtliches Zitat in deine Lösung einfügen (in Anführungszeichen und mit Zeilenangabe) oder du verweist nur indirekt auf die relevante Textstelle (mit „cf."). In der Aufgabenstellung wird verlangt, dass du Allies Gefühle zu Beginn, in der Mitte und am*

Ende ihrer Präsentation beschreibst. Diese Dreiteilung sollte sich auch in deiner Lösung widerspiegeln.

Allie's feelings at the beginning

At the beginning of her presentation Allie feels insecure and excited: "She took a deep breath. And then she began." (ll. 1/2) She appears restless, "walking up and down the stage" (l. 10), and her legs feel weak (cf. l. 10). But Allie tries to put on a brave face and hide her nervousness, hoping that "the audience wouldn't notice" (l. 11).

feelings during the presentation

While talking, her nervousness slowly disappears and she becomes more self-confident. By waving her phone in the air and starting to make jokes she wins the audience's attention (cf. ll. 18–22). She gets people involved by directly addressing them ("Ready, everyone?", l. 29) and letting them try out her app that everyone had installed when they came in. When everything works out the way she had planned it, Allie becomes much more comfortable and relaxed. She even winks at the audience (cf. l. 40) and notices that "her legs weren't shaking anymore" (l. 42).

feelings at the end

At the end of her presentation she again takes a deep breath, but this time Allie feels relieved and overjoyed that everyone is clapping. It makes her feel like being "on top of the world" (l. 52). *202 words*

3. a) ✎ *Hinweis: Bei dieser Aufgabe wird nach deiner persönlichen Meinung zu Allies App gefragt. In deiner Stellungnahme sollst du darauf eingehen, welche Chancen oder Risiken die App mit sich bringt. Beim Arbeitsauftrag „comment" musst du nicht zwingend beide Seiten gegeneinander abwägen, sondern kannst dich auch nur auf die Chancen oder Risiken konzentrieren. Darüber hinaus sollst du ausführen, welche Rolle soziale Medien generell in deinem Leben spielen und ob du persönlich Allies App* Click'd *nutzen würdest oder nicht. Mache dir am besten einige Notizen, bevor du mit dem Ausformulieren deiner Lösung beginnst. Achte auch darauf, dass du auf alle drei in der Aufgabenstellung geforderten Aspekte*

eingehst. Dazu kannst du die Aspekte zum Beispiel auf dem Angabenblatt abhaken.

In my opinion, Allie's app *Click'd* has a lot of advantages. First of all, it allows you to get to know people with the same interests really quickly and make new friends. I think this can be very helpful when you are rather shy or when you are at a party or in a new city where you don't know anybody yet. What is more, the app is very easy to use – you just need a smartphone and have to answer some questions, and there you go! I also imagine that it is great fun to find out who you share the highest score with. Of course, that means that you will only get to know people who are very much like you.

chances (and risks) of Allie's product

However, that is a general problem of social media, I think. Still, I could not do without them. I use Instagram and Facebook every day to see what my friends are doing in their free time, and to be up to date on the latest trends. I also use messenger apps like Signal and WhatsApp to chat with my friends and share photos or videos.

role social media play in your life

I would definitely like to try out *Click'd* because I would be curious to see if it would match me with the friends I already have, and because I think it is always exciting to get to know new people.

your opinion on personally using Click'd

228 words

b) *Hinweis: Bei dieser Aufgabe sollst du dir vorstellen, dass du bei Allies Präsentation der App live dabei warst und anschließend einen Bericht darüber für das Magazin des Sommercamps schreibst. Darin sollst du zunächst einige wissenswerte Fakten über* Click'd *nennen. Als Nächstes sollst du beschreiben, wie das Publikum bei der Präsentation auf die App reagiert hat. Zu guter Letzt sollst du noch deine Sichtweise auf Computer-Sommercamps für Teenager darlegen. Um dir den Einstieg zu erleichtern, ist der Anfang des Artikels bereits vorgegeben.*

Have you been "Click'd" yet?

beginning (already given)

16-year-old Allie Navarro is the winner of this year's Code Girls Camp. She has demonstrated her product in a convincing presentation to a jury of experts, other camp participants and their parents. *Click'd* is a mobile app that uses quiz questions to match people with similar interests. It is meant for anybody who wants to get to know new people and make friends.

things to know about Click'd

The audience was surprised at how easy it is to handle and how much fun it is. Allie Navarro definitely managed to convince them of the many advantages of her app. There were no signs of criticism. At the end of her presentation Allie received a big round of applause.

audience's reactions to Click'd

The positive mood during the presentation and the whole summer camp shows that camps like this can be very successful. Teenagers not only have a good time there but also learn how to use modern media and be creative – skills which they might also need in their future jobs.

view on computer summer schools for teenagers

A summer camp like the "Code Girls Camp" can change your future – just like it did with Allie Navarra, who left the camp with plenty of new friends and who told us that she is thinking about studying computer science. She has definitely been Click'd!

185 words

c) *Hinweis: Auch bei dieser Aufgabe sollst du dich in eine bestimmte Situation hineinversetzen. Stell dir vor, du bist Allie und darfst ein Jahr nach deiner Präsentation die Eröffnungsrede beim „Code Girls Camp" halten. Darin sollst du darauf eingehen, wie* Click'd *dich als Person und dein Leben verändert hat, wie du generell über das Sommercamp denkst und welchen Rat du den diesjährigen Teilnehmenden mit auf den Weg geben kannst. Achte wieder darauf, dass du in deiner Lösung alle drei Aspekte aus der Aufgabenstellung berücksichtigst. Der Anfang deiner Rede ist bereits vorgegeben.*

Hi everyone,

beginning (already given)

I'm happy to be back here at Code Girls Camp. I can't believe it's already been a year. So much has happened since then. Due to the success of my app *Click'd*, I have got in touch with people from all over the world. I have been able to share experiences with other young people who are enthusiastic about coding. Moreover, a big American computer company has got interested in my invention and has even offered me a job once I have finished school. I can say that I have become much more self-confident as a person, but I also have to be careful that all these new developments don't get too much for me.

how Click'd has changed Allie and her life

I am very thankful to the organisers of this camp and everyone else that they opened up this opportunity for me. And thank you for having me here as a speaker and for your enthusiasm about me and my app. I am very curious to know how things will develop this year and what new inventions you will present to the jury at the end of the camp.

how she feels about the summer camp in general

Finally, may I give you some advice? Believe in your ideas! Never give up when things don't run smoothly! Be creative! And above all: get Click'd! Try to get in touch with others who share the same interests and then work together to turn your ideas into reality.

her advice for the new participants

Thank you for listening! Good luck! *214 words*

Erster Prüfungsteil: Hörverstehen

Hörverstehen Teil 1: A *hockey lesson*

1. c) … several times a week.
   Hinweis: "Simone had been shocked to see on her timetable that there were four periods of PE a week." (Z. 1/2)

2. c) … worried.
   Hinweis: "She was getting nervous." (Z. 4)

3. b) … take sports seriously.
   Hinweis: "I want you to work just as hard here as you do for your university entrance or anything else you do." (Z. 9/10)

4. a) … numbers the students.
   Hinweis: "'Okay,' she said, running down the room and counting the girls off. 'One, two, one, two. Team one is playing against team two,' she said." (Z. 12/13)

5. a) … bigger.
   Hinweis: "Simone was looking out at the huge playing fields. There was a running track, several tennis courts, hockey fields. The grass ran on for what seemed like miles down towards the sea. […] Absolutely nothing like the grey asphalt field at her old school." (Z. 15–18)

6. b) … no experience.
   Hinweis: "Simone opened her mouth to say that she had never played hockey before." (Z. 22/23)

7. b) … observes the students.
   Hinweis: "Miss James was right in the middle of the teams seeing who could play and had talent or who hated it and was too lazy." (Z. 27/28)

8. c) … is terrified.
   Hinweis: "She started to panic." (Z. 30)

9. c) ... automatically.
Hinweis: "Without thinking, Simone threw herself and her stick at the ball and pushed it back out into the field." (Z. 33/34)

10. c) ... talented player.
Hinweis: "But as the game continued it became clear to her that her goal-keeping skills weren't an accident. She was good at guessing when the ball was coming towards her and from what angle." (Z. 36–38)

Hörverstehen Teil 2: *Conkers: A traditional seasonal game*

1. a) ... a coming competition.
Hinweis: "She's helping to organise the Irish Conker Championship which takes place here in the park in two weeks." (Z. 4/5)

2. c) ... against another person.
Hinweis: "Oh, the game is played by two players." (Z. 8)

3. c) ... attack a conker.
Hinweis: "The other player swings their own conker and tries to hit the first player's conker." (Z. 12/13)

4. a) ... to pieces.
Hinweis: "Basically, they take turns hitting each other's conkers until one finally breaks." (Z. 13/14)

5. a) ... old conkers.
Hinweis: "You can leave it in a dry place for about a year and that will make it harder." (Z. 18/19)

6. b) ... hundreds of years ago.
Hinweis: "Well, playing conkers goes all the way back to the late 15th century." (Z. 22/23)

7. b) ... dangerous activity.
Hinweis: "But many schools have banned conkers because head teachers are afraid that children might get hurt while playing the game." (Z. 30–32)

8. c) ... get people into the fresh air.
Hinweis: "So, we're trying to bring back the outdoors, if you like." (Z. 36/37)

9. a) … should have some skill.
   Hinweis: "No, all you need is a good steady hand." (Z. 43)

Zweiter Prüfungsteil: Leseverstehen – Wortschatz – Schreiben

Leseverstehen: *The power of traditional beliefs*

1. b) … trouble.
   Evidence: an itchy nose is a sign of an upcoming fight
   Hinweis: Z. 6

2. true
   Evidence: Itching on the inner side of your hands – a sign of money to come.
   Hinweis: Z. 10/11

3. b) … honesty.
   Evidence: A black spot on the tongue is a sign of telling lies. /
   "Stick your tongue out so I can see if you're lying".
   Hinweis: Z. 14–16

4. c) … other people think of you.
   Evidence: If it's the right ear that feels extremely warm, people are talking about you positively, but if it's the left ear, the talk is negative.
   Hinweis: Z. 17/18

5. false
   Evidence: the word for superstition is *piseog* / everything connected with magic is believed to be a *piseog*
   Hinweis: Z. 19–21

6. c) … cause problems for them.
   Evidence: If you didn't find these things, your luck would turn bad.
   Hinweis: Z. 25/26

7. true
   Evidence: they show our psychological needs / they show how we as humans have thought, felt, and interacted
   ✎ *Hinweis: Z. 30/31*

8. c) … are practiced regularly.
   Evidence: they survived because of repetition / When something is done again and again, […] it becomes […] a tradition.
   ✎ *Hinweis: Z. 33–36*

9. true
   Evidence: each new family creates their own rituals
   ✎ *Hinweis: Z. 37/38*

10. a) … choose what to think.
    Evidence: it's up to you to decide what to believe in
    ✎ *Hinweis: Z. 40/41*

Wortschatz: *Food as a cultural experience*

1. b) … connection …
2. c) … come to …
3. taste / smell / flavour / …
4. ill / sick / weak / down / sad / depressed / bad / …
5. dishes / meals / recipes / spices / ingredients / influences / …
6. d) … variety …
7. traditions / culture / …
8. c) … manage …
9. shops / stores / restaurants / …
10. a) …generally …
11. served / sold / offered / found / available / …
12. delicious / tasty / yummy / fantastic / great / typical / …
13. b) … unites …

Schreiben: *Do you speak chocolate?*

Hinweis: Im Prüfungsteil „Schreiben" wird dir ein Text vorgelegt und du musst drei Aufgaben dazu bearbeiten. Gehe am besten folgendermaßen vor: Lies dir den Ausgangstext einmal vollständig durch, damit du weißt, worum es geht. Sieh dir anschließend die Aufgaben dazu an. Bei der ersten Aufgabe sollst du den Text (bzw. bestimmte Aspekte daraus) zusammenfassen. Bei der zweiten Aufgabe musst du den Text analysieren und deine Untersuchungsergebnisse anhand von Textbelegen untermauern. Bei der dritten Aufgabe kannst du zwischen mehreren Themen auswählen. In diesem Fall hast du die Möglichkeit, entweder eine Erörterung zum Thema des Texts zu schreiben (Teilaufgabe a), die Geschichte fortzusetzen (Teilaufgabe b) oder aber einen Artikel für die Homepage der Schule zu verfassen (Teilaufgabe c). Überlege, zu welchem Thema dir am meisten einfällt und welche Art des Schreibens dir eher liegt (kreativ oder sachlich-erörternd). Entscheide dich dann für eine Teilaufgabe und bleibe bei dieser – du solltest, wenn möglich, nicht zwischendurch „umschwenken", da dich das wertvolle Zeit kostet.

1. *Hinweis: Bei dieser Aufgabe sollst du beschreiben, in welcher Situation sich Jaz und ihre Mitschülerinnen befinden und wie sie mit dieser Situation umgehen. Überfliege zunächst den Text noch einmal und unterstreiche relevante Stellen, damit du keinen wichtigen Aspekt übersiehst. Im ersten Teil deiner Lösung solltest du erwähnen, dass Nadima eine neue Schülerin aus Syrien ist, dass Jaz und ihre Mitschülerinnen versuchen, sich mit ihr zu unterhalten, sich die Kommunikation aber schwierig gestaltet, weil Nadima kein Englisch spricht. Im zweiten Teil gehst du dann auf die unterschiedlichen Strategien ein, mit denen die Mädchen versuchen, sich mit Nadima zu verständigen. Jaz' Klassenkameradinnen überhäufen Nadima mit Fragen und probieren es mit Google Translate, haben damit aber keinen Erfolg und verlieren schnell das Interesse an einem Gespräch mit Nadima. Jaz ist geduldiger und versucht es zunächst mit Deutsch und Französisch, greift dann aber auf eine Geste (anstelle von Worten) zurück, indem sie Nadima ein Stück Schokolade anbietet.*

   the situation Jaz and her classmates are in

   Jaz, the main character of the story, and several of her schoolmates gather outside the school canteen. They all surround Nadima, a new student and refugee from Syria. Jaz's schoolmates Kara, Chloe, Lily and Elly try to communicate with Nadima. But very soon it becomes obvious that this is difficult, because Nadima does not speak any English at all.

At first the girls shower the new schoolmate with questions, but without any success. Jaz, by contrast, tries to create understanding for Nadima's situation and asks for more patience. Then the girls have the idea of using Google Translate, but this does not work out either because they cannot find out the country Nadima comes from and which language she speaks. They soon lose interest in Nadima and leave the scene.

how they deal with the situation

Only Jaz stays with Nadima. She tries to speak to her in French and German, but still without any success. Finally Jaz chooses a completely different way of getting in touch with Nadima, by offering her some chocolate. This time, she gets an immediate response: Nadima not only eats the chocolate, but offers Jaz some sweets in return. *188 words*

2. *Hinweis: Bei dieser Aufgabe sollst du erklären, was man im Textauszug über Jaz' Charakter erfährt. Lies den Text noch einmal gründlich von Anfang an durch und unterstreiche alle Stellen, an denen es darum geht, wie Jaz sich verhält und was sie sagt. Überlege, was diese Stellen über sie als Person aussagen und notiere dir passende Adjektive oder Überbegriffe am Rand. Beim Ausformulieren der Lösung kannst du dann auf deine Notizen und Unterstreichungen zurückgreifen: Beginne jeden Absatz damit, dass du zunächst eine von Jaz' Eigenschaften nennst und anschließend Beispiele dafür aus dem Text anführst. Du kannst entweder mit direkten Zitaten arbeiten oder aber indirekt auf bestimmte Textstellen verweisen. Am elegantesten ist es, wenn du zwischen verschiedenen Arten des Zitieren abwechselst.*

The situation in front of the canteen reveals quite a lot about Jaz's character.

introductory sentence

First of all, it becomes obvious that Jaz is a very empathetic girl who understands what Nadima must be feeling. For example, when Kara talks very slowly and loudly to Nadima, Jaz realises that this might make Nadima feel stupid and steps in by saying "I don't think she's deaf" (l. 12). When the other girls keep on showering Nadima with questions, Jaz senses that this might

main part – Jaz's character traits: empathy

be too much for Nadima and tries to defend her: "Give her a break. It's obvious she can't understand a word you're saying." (ll. 19/20).

Moreover, Jaz appears to be a strong and courageous person. She not only opposes her classmates when they behave in an insensitive way towards Nadima. She is also the only one who stays with Nadima, even though both of them feel uneasy in the situation at first (cf. ll. 40/41). *courage*

Last but not least, Jaz also turns out to have good social skills, because she manages to solve the communication problem in a creative way. For example, she uses body language to cheer Nadima up: "She just stood there looking puzzled. I gave her a big smile and raised my shoulders in a big comedy shrug. She smiled and did a big shrug back." (ll. 34/35). The ice finally breaks when Jaz offers Nadima a piece of chocolate. This simple gesture gives Nadima the possibility to enter into a dialogue with Jaz: The look on Nadima's face changes ("Her eyes seemed to come to life.", l. 50) and she offers Jaz some sweets in return (cf. ll. 51/52). *274 words* *good social skills*

3. a) ✎ *Hinweis: Bei dieser Aufgabe geht es um die entscheidende Geste am Schluss des Textes, als Jaz Nadima ein Stück Schokolade anbietet. Du sollst erörtern, welche Wirkung dieser Moment auf Nadima haben könnte, warum die Schokolade eine so wichtige Rolle im Text spielt und wie du persönlich Jaz' Verhalten in der Situation bewertest. Notiere dir am besten zu jedem der drei Aspekte ein paar Stichpunkte, bevor du mit dem Ausformulieren beginnst – so stellst du sicher, dass du keinen wichtigen Punkt vergisst.*

At the end of the extract, Jaz manages to overcome the communication problem with Nadima, the girl from Syria, by means of a simple gesture. *introductory sentence*

By using body language instead of words, Jaz tries to look for a code that is understood in both cultures. A smile, for example, is seen as an expression of *why the chocolate plays an important role in the text*

sympathy and kindness by most people around the world. The same goes for sharing food: When Jaz offers Nadima a piece of chocolate, this is easy to understand as a sign of friendship. Moreover, it is a way of communication that allows Nadima to switch from a passive to an active role. She is no longer just the outsider who is talked to and does not understand, but can offer Jaz some sweets, too.

how Nadima might feel about Jaz's behaviour

Jaz's determination, the fact that she does not give up and lose interest in Nadima (like the other girls do), must have a deep impact on Nadima. The girl from Syria may not understand English, but she understands that Jaz stays with her and keeps trying to make contact with her. Nadima must definitely get the feeling that Jaz is interested in her as a person, and that they might even become friends.

what you think about Jaz's action

In my opinion, Jaz's empathy and her creativity in the situation are very impressive. She is successful in finding a way of communicating and making Nadima feel welcome even without using words. Jaz shows us that it is possible to create understanding even if we do not speak the same language, and that tiny gestures can make a huge difference. *262 words*

b) *Hinweis: Bei dieser Aufgabe sollst du eine Fortsetzung der Geschichte schreiben. Dazu sollst du dir vorstellen, Jaz' Eltern möchten die neue Freundin ihrer Tochter kennenlernen und laden Nadima zu sich nach Hause zum Abendessen ein. Du sollst darauf eingehen, wie Jaz, ihre Familie und Nadima mit der Sprachbarriere umgehen, was Jaz unternimmt, damit sich Nadima wohlfühlt, und wie Nadima am Ende die Sympathien aller gewinnt. Mache dir zunächst einige Stichpunkte und achte beim Ausformulieren darauf, dass deine Fortsetzung sowohl sprachlich als auch inhaltlich gut zum Ausgangstext passt. Du musst den Abend aus der Sicht der Ich-Erzählerin Jaz beschreiben und solltest auch immer wieder Dialoge in deinen Text einstreuen. Beachte, dass der Beginn der Lösung bereits vorgegeben ist und du den angefangenen Satz aus der Aufgabenstellung fortsetzen musst.*

Mum and Dad were already busy setting the table. Nadima just stood in the doorway to our kitchen. I saw Nadima taking a deep breath and

beginning (already given)

then she entered the room.

"Please, come in! Take a seat and make yourself at home," my mum said to her warmly.

Nadima sat down and looked around the room. She discovered the photos of my family on the wall, particularly the one of me when I was a baby. She looked at me with a smile and I replied, "Yes, that's me! I was cute, wasn't I?" Nadima nodded and laughed.

"So, for how long have you been here?", my dad wanted to start the conversation.

problem with communication

Nadima looked at me with a questioning face.

"Dad, Nadima doesn't speak much English yet. You can either use your smartphone to translate or you might have to communicate in a different way, for example by using your hands."

Jaz explaining in order to help Nadima feel more comfortable

"Oh, sorry, I forgot that", Dad replied.

My mum put the bowls with the meat, potatoes and beans on the table.

"Thank you!" Nadima said.

"Oh, you're very welcome." Mum answered.

She took Nadima's plate and first put the beans, then the potatoes and the meat on it.

At this moment my father started making noises: "Baa, baa, baaaaa!" pointing to the meat on Nadima's plate.

Jaz's dad's attempt to solve the communication problem

"Dad, you're embarrassing", I said angrily.

But to my surprise Nadima started laughing and gave us a "thumbs up". I realised that Nadima understood that the meat was lamb. Meat that she knew from home. Everyone laughed.

"Enjoy your meal", my mother said slowly.

"Enjoy your meal", answered Nadima, still a bit insecure.

Then she said the same phrase in Arabic, her native language, and we repeated after her. My dad, in particular, tried really hard to get the pronunciation right, and Nadima was patient when teaching him. Both of them beamed with pride when he managed to say it correctly.

Nadima winning everyone's sympathy

From that moment on, the ice had been broken, and we made it a game teaching each other words and phrases in both languages. Nadima had won my parents' sympathy, and the other way around too.

329 words

c) ✎ *Hinweis: Stell dir vor, Jaz möchte einen „food bazaar" an der Schule organisieren – also eine Veranstaltung, bei der Gerichte aus verschiedenen Ländern und Kulturen angeboten werden. Sie schreibt einen Artikel für die Homepage der Schule, in dem sie berichtet, wie sie auf die Idee für das Projekt gekommen ist, wie Essen Menschen aus verschiedenen Kulturen zusammenbringen kann, und wie sie den Basar organisieren möchte. Die Überschrift und der Anfang des Artikels ist bereits vorgegeben. Achte darauf, dass sich deine Lösung möglichst nahtlos daran anschließt und dass du keinen der Aspekte aus der Aufgabenstellung vergisst.*

Bringing cultures together through food

beginning (already given)

When I first met Nadima, the new girl from Syria at our school, we had trouble communicating with words, but "talked" to each other through food. This made me think

that eating food and having a meal together is far more than defeating hunger. In any culture in the world, offering food is seen as a sign of hospitality. Being invited for dinner is a gesture of friendship. When I offered Nadima some chocolate, this was the moment the ice between us was broken. It was a common "language" we both understood and that

how food can play a role in bringing different cultures together gave Nadima the self-confidence to enter the conversation by offering me sweets, too.

The sweets that looked like Turkish Delight were very delicious. I had never tried them before, but I liked them and became curious about the country Nadima came from.

how Jaz got the idea to organise the food bazaar

A few days later, an idea came to my mind: Why not share the experience Nadima and I made and organise a food bazaar? There are students from many different countries and cultural backgrounds at our school. Often however, we do not really know a lot about each other. At the bazaar, everyone – students, parents and teachers – could bring their favourite dishes or specialties from their country. By sitting together, sharing a meal, talking and laughing together, we could get to know each other better. I am convinced that the bazaar will be a great opportunity to broaden our horizons and to strengthen the sense of community at our school.

how food can play a role in bringing different cultures together

If you are interested, you are very much invited to join the organising team. We are going to meet for the first time on Tuesday, May 25 from 6 to 7 pm at the school canteen. Together with our head teacher Ms Jain, we will decide on a date for the bazaar. We are also going to brainstorm what tasks need to be done and who would like to do them – from designing flyers in order to promote the event, to decorating the tables on the day of the bazaar, etc.

how Jaz wants to organise the food bazaar at school

Probably, some work will have to be done, but seeing all the happy faces will certainly be worth the effort.

Please, do join us. I hope to see you all there!

338 words

Erster Prüfungsteil: Hörverstehen

Hörverstehen Teil 1: *Voices from New Zealand*

1. b) … in the Māori language.
   Hinweis: "The New Zealand popstar has released an album of five songs translated into Māori …" (Z. 2/3)

2. b) … sports event.
   Hinweis: "When she was asked to sing New Zealand's national anthem at the Rugby World Cup that year, …" (Z. 8/9)

3. b) … negatively.
   Hinweis: "They were very angry at her for using her native language." (Z. 11/12)

4. a) … honour something.
   Hinweis: "With her Māori version, Hinewehi wanted to celebrate her culture." (Z. 12/13)

5. b) … a debate.
   Hinweis: "The result was a national discussion about New Zealand's history as a British colony and how it continues to harm the Māori and their language even today." (Z. 14–16)

6. a) … a cooperation project.
   Hinweis: "Hinewehi has continued to fight for her native language […]. In 2019, she recorded an album of songs in Māori together with both Māori and non-Māori musicians." (Z. 17–19)

7. c) … an important award.
   Hinweis: "In 2021, Queen Elizabeth II even gave her the Order of New Zealand …" (Z. 19/20)

8. a) … learn Māori.
   Hinweis: "The idea is to teach more New Zealanders the language across the country." (Z. 25)

9. b) … quite low.
   ✎ *Hinweis: "By 1980, very few Māori people could still speak the language, just under 20 % of them." (Z. 28/29)*

Hörverstehen Teil 2: *New Zealand Rugby Museum*

1. b) … rugby testing zone.
   ✎ *Hinweis: "We've got a small area for trying out your rugby skills." (Z. 6)*

2. b) … 1885.
   ✎ *Hinweis: "Well, our oldest rugby shirt is from 1885." (Z. 10)*

3. b) … a few important objects.
   ✎ *Hinweis: "Interestingly, one of our colleagues suggested that we take some of the valuable items and make copies of them." (Z. 15–17)*

4. c) … in the same city.
   ✎ *Hinweis: "So we did some research on the 1905 All Blacks rugby shirt and we found that it had been made by an old factory which still exists here in Palmerston North." (Z. 17–19)*

5. a) … a bit tight.
   ✎ *Hinweis: "But you have to be very slim to fit in this one comfortably." (Z. 24/25)*

6. c) … rugby was great for coming together.
   ✎ *Hinweis: "It was your excuse to get off the farm and meet people." (Z. 31/32)*

7. a) … could afford it.
   ✎ *Hinweis: "It was also a big factor that it was such a cheap sport to take part in …" (Z. 33/34)*

8. b) … failed to make rugby popular.
   ✎ *Hinweis: "… the All Blacks tried to introduce rugby to the USA. And unfortunately, they won a little bit too easily in the nine games, and that was the end of American rugby." (Z. 38–40)*

9. c) … bit of cloth.
   ✎ *Hinweis: "I do have a favourite, actually, I was thinking about it just before this interview: It's a little piece of the first All Blacks rugby shirt." (Z. 43/44)*

Zweiter Prüfungsteil: Leseverstehen – Wortschatz – Schreiben

Leseverstehen: *A travel blog*

1. c) … share the name of the kiwifruit.
   Evidence: People wonder: "Why are New Zealanders called after a fruit?"
   Hinweis: Z. 4/5

2. b) … clear up a common misunderstanding.
   Evidence: it's time we explain things for our international readers
   Hinweis: Z. 6

3. a) … huge.
   Evidence: they lay massive eggs / they have the biggest eggs in the world / a kiwi egg is about six times heavier than a chicken egg!
   Hinweis: Z. 10–13

4. a) … when it's dark.
   Evidence: Kiwis spend the day sleeping and hunt at night.
   Hinweis: Z. 14

5. b) … safe home in the past.
   Evidence: kiwis lived for a long time without any major predators / without any real threats, there was no need to fly
   Hinweis: Z. 18–20

6. a) … people's pets.
   Evidence: the kiwis' environment has changed a lot because humans settled on the island and brought animals with them / A single dog can wipe out all the kiwis in one area
   Hinweis: Z. 21/22 und Z. 24/25

7. b) … uncertain.
   Evidence: kiwis may disappear from New Zealand in our lifetime. / Luckily, things are improving for some kiwi populations. / In controlled areas where kiwis live free from predators, their numbers are slowly increasing.
   Hinweis: Z. 26–28

8. a) ... just fine.
   Evidence: But can you call us 'Kiwis'? Absolutely! / you're welcome to call us Kiwis / it's hard to imagine being called anything else
   Hinweis: Z. 29/30, Z. 32–34

9. c) ... the military.
   Evidence: The kiwi bird was first seen on the badges of soldiers
   Hinweis: Z. 34

10. a) ... looks like the bird.
    Evidence: it was soon renamed 'kiwifruit' due to its similarity to the kiwi bird / both are brown and fluffy
    Hinweis: Z. 37–39

Wortschatz: *Freaks?*

1. c) ... crazy about ...
2. b) ... habit ...
3. said / confessed / admitted / stated / explained / ...
4. stress / panic / nervousness / frustration / unease / pressure / anxiety/ ...
5. d) ... control ...
6. struggling / dealing / diagnosed / affected / ...
7. a) ... with ...
8. easy / funny / amusing / cool / ...
9. a) ... conclusions ...
10. b) ... sure ...
11. check / look at / ...
12. compassion / sympathy/ understanding / kindness / ...
13. normal / happy / good / fulfilling / ...

Schreiben: *Lost Numbers*

Hinweis: Der Prüfungsteil „Schreiben" besteht aus drei Aufgaben. In Teil 1 (Aufgabe zur Sicherung des Textverständnisses) musst du in der Regel wesentliche Inhalte des Ausgangstextes in deinen eigenen Worten zusammenfassen. In Teil 2 (Aufgabe zur grundlegenden Interpretation) musst du den Text auf bestimmte Aspekte hin genauer untersuchen. In Teil 3 hast du eine Wahlmöglichkeit zwischen zwei Themen: einer sachlich-erörternden oder einer kreativen Aufgabe.
Lies dir den Ausgangstext zunächst einmal gründlich durch, um dir einen Überblick über den Inhalt zu verschaffen. Sieh dir dann die Aufgabenstellungen an. Gehe den Text für jede Aufgabe noch einmal genau durch und unterstreiche die jeweils relevanten Stellen. Mache dir ggf. am Rand Notizen in deinen eigenen Worten – diese helfen dir beim anschließenden Ausformulieren deiner Lösung.

1. *Hinweis: Bei dieser Aufgabe sollst du beschreiben, in welcher Situation sich Felix befindet und wie er damit umgeht. Deine Lösung sollte also zweigeteilt sein. Gehe zunächst darauf ein, dass Felix auf dem Weg zur Schule immer seine Schritte zählt und dabei Musik hört. Diesmal wird er allerdings von Mitschülern bei seiner Routine gestört. Er reagiert darauf, indem er wieder nach Hause zurückgeht, um von vorn mit dem Zählen zu beginnen. Daher kommt er am Ende zu spät in den Unterricht und muss nachsitzen.*

Felix, the protagonist of the story, leads a difficult life due to his compulsive behaviour. A situation in which this becomes particularly noticeable is when he walks to school. Felix has to count his steps, exactly 1,000 steps to reach school, while listening to the right music. *Felix's situation*

One morning, a group of other students approach Felix and laugh at him. Felix doesn't listen to what they say and simply walks faster. Then, however, he realises that he has lost his numbers. As he is worried that something bad might happen if he does not stick to his usual routine, he is forced to go back home and count his steps again. That is why he eventually arrives late for school and gets detention, which he accepts without complaining. When his classmate Bindi asks him why he is late, Felix hides the true reason and pretends to have forgotten something at home. *how Felix deals with his situation*

151 words

2. *Hinweis: Bei dieser Aufgabe sollst du Felix' Persönlichkeit untersuchen. Gehe den Text noch einmal ganz genau durch und unterstreiche alle Stellen, an denen zum Ausdruck kommt, wie Felix sich verhält, welche Gedanken ihm durch den Kopf gehen und wie er seine Umgebung wahrnimmt. Überlege dir anschließend, was das über seine Persönlichkeit aussagt, und finde passende Oberbegriffe, mit denen du seine Eigenschaften beschreiben kannst. Beim Ausformulieren deiner Lösung solltest du jeden Absatz so aufbauen, dass du zunächst eine Eigenschaft nennst und anschließend Belege dafür aus dem Text anführst. Das kannst du mithilfe von direkten Textzitaten tun oder aber mit indirekten Textverweisen.*

Felix is a character with many different sides to his personality.

compulsive behaviour and thinking

The first noticeable aspect is that he seems to be caught up in strict routines and compulsions which strongly influence his behaviour and way of thinking. For example, he is forced to count his steps to school, following the same routine day by day. Everything has to happen in a particular way – he has to take his "usual step", put on the "right music" and "time it exactly" to arrive at school (ll. 4/5).

intelligence and lack of self-confidence

Secondly, it also becomes clear that Felix is very intelligent and self-critical. He is painfully aware that others make fun of him (cf. ll. 22/23) and therefore lacks self-confidence, calling himself "the weirdest sixteen-year-old-guy in the universe" (ll. 1/2).

difficulties in social interactions

Moreover, he seems to be somewhat of an outsider at school and to have problems socialising. This becomes obvious when he says, "I wish someone would tell me what the rules are for talking to people so I can learn them" (ll. 39/40). He also walks to school on his own wearing headphones, perhaps so that he doesn't have to talk to other people.

sensitivity and attention to "small things"

Last but not least, Felix is also a very sensitive person who pays attention to "little things", such as the beauty of nature, which many of his schoolmates probably wouldn't notice. For example, he observes how the sunlight reflects in the dew (cf. l. 13) and what his family's house looks like in the morning sun (cf. ll. 31/32).

248 words

3. a) ✎ *Hinweis: Bei dieser Aufgabe musst du zu einem Zitat aus dem Text Stellung beziehen. In der Aufgabenstellung sind drei inhaltliche Aspekte angegeben, auf die du dabei besonders eingehen sollst – nämlich welchen Stellenwert Regeln für Felix haben, welche Rolle sie für dich persönlich spielen und ob/ inwieweit sie für die Gesellschaft als Ganzes nützlich sind. Bevor du mit dem Ausformulieren deiner Lösung beginnst, solltest du dir kurz ein paar Stichpunkte notieren, was du zu jedem der genannten Aspekte schreiben könntest. Deine Lösung kannst du beispielsweise in drei größere inhaltliche Abschnitte unterteilen, in denen sich die Dreiteilung aus der Aufgabenstellung widerspiegelt. Versuche, deine Gedanken und Argumente jeweils mit konkreten Beispielen zu belegen.*

importance of rules for Felix (I)

For Felix, the narrator of the story, rules are an absolute must. In his opinion, strictly following fixed rules makes life easier for himself and everyone.
Felix likes rules (such as the fact that you get detention for being late) because they give him a feeling of security: they apply to everyone and you know exactly what to expect. This makes life and social interactions much more predictable.

importance of rules in own life

In my life, rules play an important part as well – at home, at school, and in my free time. For example, my parents set rules as to when I have to be back home when I go out in the evening. At school, there are rules that say that cheating on tests is not allowed. And when I play soccer with friends, everyone follows the same rules of the game.
I would agree with Felix that rules can serve as guidelines and that it is usually good to follow them.

usefulness of rules in society in general

Moreover, rules are important for society in general because without them there would be chaos. Just imagine everyone making up their own traffic rules!

However, in my opinion, there are also exceptions when it is okay or even necessary not to follow the rules – for example, when they are unfair, discriminate against someone, or don't make any sense at all.

importance of rules for Felix (II)

Felix also has certain inner "rules" that only he knows; for example, that he has to count his steps to school to avoid having a bad day. These rules give him the feeling of being in control of his life; however, in reality, the rules control him, because he gets panicked whenever he can't follow them. Thus, he is no longer free to make his own decisions, but is a slave of the rules and suffers from them.

conclusion

To sum it all up, I agree with Felix that rules are important for living together, but it is also not necessary to follow them blindly. *322 words*

b) *Hinweis: Bei dieser Aufgabe sollst du eine Fortsetzung der Geschichte schreiben. Auch hier sind wieder drei inhaltliche Aspekte vorgegeben, die in deiner Lösung enthalten sein müssen: Felix' Erklärung für sein Verhalten, Bindis Reaktion darauf und ihr Rat an Felix. Notiere dir zu jedem der drei Aspekte zunächst einige Stichpunkte: Wie könnte Felix sich wohl fühlen, als er Bindi sein Geheimnis verrät, und was könnte er sagen? Wird Bindi Verständnis haben für Felix oder reagiert sie eher ablehnend? Was wird sie Felix empfehlen, wie er mit seinem Geheimnis umgehen soll – es für sich behalten, sich weiteren Personen anvertrauen, sich Unterstützung suchen oder etwas ganz anderes? Achte dann beim Ausformulieren deiner Lösung darauf, dass dein Text zum Rest der Geschichte passt – du musst also aus der Ich-Perspektive von Felix schreiben und in der Zeitform des „simple past". Um deinen Text möglichst lebendig zu gestalten, kannst du immer wieder auch direkte Rede einstreuen.*
Als Hilfestellung für deinen Text ist der erste Satz bereits vorgegeben.

beginning (already given)

Bindi caught up with me when we walked out of the classroom. She asked me to follow her to the cafeteria and we sat down together. Then she asked me directly: "Felix, what was it that you had to get from home so urgently this morning? And why you didn't even protest when Mr Campbell gave you detention?"

I felt uncomfortable and wanted to get up from the table. But Bindi insisted and made me sit down again. "I'd really like to understand, Felix."

She looked at me as if she really meant it. Eventually I came up with the truth.

"I know, you'll think I'm kidding, but … I went back to find the lost numbers." *Felix's explanation*

Bindi asked me with a puzzled look: "I'm not really sure I understand. What does that mean?"

So I told her in detail about my situation. "I need to count my steps on the way to school. If I don't do it, I know it'll be a miserable day. I have to do it, I really can't help it. I don't want something bad to happen."

Bindi looked at me with compassion. *Bindi's reaction*

"I see … you don't really have a choice, do you? That must be quite hard sometimes."

"I've never told anyone about my situation – Sam and the others just think I'm weird."

We sat for a moment in silence, then Bindi said: "You know, for me you're not weird at all. I'm happy you told me about it – now I know much better what is going on in your mind. And I think Sam and the others can understand as well. A lot of people have similar thoughts – my mum, for example, has to check three times if she has locked the door whenever we leave the house."

Then, Bindi came up with the idea that I could give a short presentation in class about my situation. Together, we planned the presentation during the following two weeks, after informing our class teacher. Sam Birch kept on making stupid comments every now and then after that – but now there was always someone who told him to shut up, and so his bullying finally stopped altogether. *349 words*

Bindi's advice

Lösungen zu
Zentrale Prüfungen 2024 – Englisch
Anforderungen für den Mittleren Schulabschluss (MSA)

Um dir die Lösungen zur Prüfung 2024 schnellstmöglich zur Verfügung stellen zu können, bringen wir sie in digitaler Form heraus.

Sobald die Original-Prüfungsaufgaben 2024 freigegeben sind, können die dazugehörigen Lösungen als PDF auf der Plattform **MySTARK** heruntergeladen werden (Zugangscode vgl. Umschlaginnenseite).

Aktuelle Prüfung

www.stark-verlag.de/mystark

PRÜFUNGS-
ANGST

STOPP DIE PANIK

Mit der Fußsohlen-Methode

Prüfungen können Angst- und Fluchtsituationen sein. Dein Körper schüttet Adrenalin aus und dämpft das Gefühl in den Füßen. Z. B. beim Weglaufen ist es gut, wenn man die Füße nicht spürt. Eine Prüfung ist aber **keine Gefahrensituation**. Signalisiere deinem Körper, dass du nicht weglaufen musst, und bring das Gefühl in deine Füße zurück:

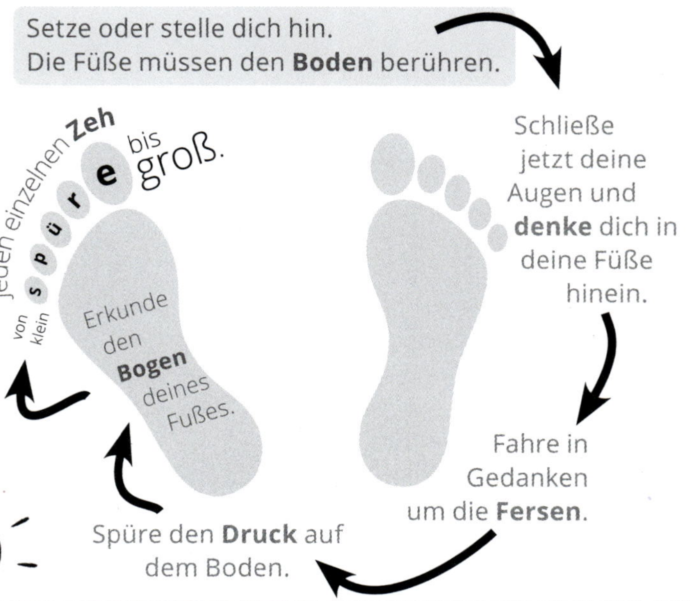

Dein Körper **fühlt** die Füße wieder und denkt, er sei in keiner Panik-Situation, sondern in **Sicherheit**.